Arab Issues: Historical Approaches to the Arab Spring,
Human Rights and Other Middle East Concerns

ARAB ISSUES

*Historical Approaches
to the Arab Spring,
Human Rights and Other
Middle East Concerns*

Professor Dr. Saad Abudayeh

Westphalia Press
An Imprint of the Policy Studies Organization
Washington, DC

ARAB ISSUES: HISTORICAL APPROACHES TO THE ARAB SPRING,
HUMAN RIGHTS AND OTHER MIDDLE EAST CONCERNS

All Rights Reserved © 2024 by Policy Studies Organization

Westphalia Press
An imprint of Policy Studies Organization
1367 Connecticut Avenue NW
Washington, D.C. 20036
info@ipsonet.org

ISBN: 978-1-63723-528-7

Cover and interior design by Jeffrey Barnes
jbarnesbook.design

Daniel Gutierrez-Sandoval, Executive Director
PSO and Westphalia Press

Updated material and comments on this edition
can be found at the Westphalia Press website:
www.westphaliapress.org

Dedication

*To my sincere Saudi friend, Mohammed A. Al-Theeb
and to my cousin, Marwan K. S. Abudayeh*

Table of Contents

PART 1

CHAPTER 1

The Texts, Expressions, and Causes of Arab Spring in Tunisia, Egypt, and Libya

Summary

The expressions and texts which appeared with the so-called Arab Spring reflect the real causes of the Arab Spring in the eyes of the people. The Arab language is full of expressions and colloquialisms. By the beginning of 2011, for the first time in the recent Arab history, pressure groups started the Arab Spring in Tunisia. The pressure groups in the Arab world moved to overthrow the regimes, putting pressure on governments to change. However, this time the phenomenon radiated outwards, extending from Tunisia to Egypt, then Yemen, Bahrain, and Libya. The movement started in the Arab world in Africa; 72% of the area of the Arab world and two-thirds of all Arabs live in North Africa.

The inspiring sacrifice of El Boazeezi, which launched the shake up, was exported to other Arab States and became a phenomenon among individuals who started to imitate and burn themselves like El Boazeezi. This extended to the Arab states and there were small cases of the influence reaching Europe. All these individuals who protested and burnt themselves shouted that they were being mistreated by their government during their acts of protest. Thus, facing injustice or humiliation is a common factor between El Boazeezi and others who did the same thing and used the same method to express their dissatisfactions and frustrations. All the others who burnt themselves shared with (El Boazeezi) the following things:

1. Being humiliated by corrupted regimes.
2. Being unemployed and frustrated by the government.

Introduction

Pressure Groups in Political Science are different from parties. They don't want to rule, they don't have a cadre and employees, and they don't receive foreign support from the outside. *The combination of the word "corruption" and other words which caused the shake up*—several combining factors lead to this situation. The most important factors were unemployment, poverty, and corruption. There is one factor in our point of view which helped increase the frustration of the people—the collapse of the *image* of the governments and rulers and the *legitimacy* of the Arab rulers, especially those who were accused of a lack of nationalism. Their legitimacy was shaken as the Constitutional party had lost its legitimacy in Tunisia and the people in Tunisia still demanded to have new rulers—no one from the ex-party. The priority in Egypt was similar to that in Tunisia in facing corruption, which was a common factor. This corruption was further exposed after the collapse of the President Mubarak. The businessmen were ruling the country in the same manner they were running their businesses. Leaders had great confidence and they lost all motivation to reform—they were very confident that they were protected and immune. This study discusses the combinations of causes which were behind the so called Arab Spring and focuses on new expressions and phenomena that accompanied the so-called Arab Spring.

The Expressions and Texts

The expressions and texts which appeared with the so-called Arab Spring reflect the real causes of the Arab Spring in the eyes of the people. The Arab language is full of expressions and colloquialisms. The Miracle of the Prophet Mohammad (PUH) in the Holy Quran related to the language and the rhetoric of God in the Holy Quran. As Ahmed Ali wrote in his introduction when he translated the Quran into English, Quran Arabic is distinguished by sublimity and excellence of sound and eloquence, rhetoric and metaphor, assonance and alliteration, and onomatopoeias of sound and rhythm (1). The Society in Mecca was linguistically advanced. Therefore, language was the best means to attract and convert the non-believers. We observed that the Arabs have been concerned with utilizing the appropriate choice of words in politics or their social life. In national or historical occasions, they use the expressions of the wars and their results. The result of the 1948 war with Israel, for instance, wasn't in the favor of the Arabs. They called it EL NAKBAH which means disaster. They called the results of the 1967 War— EL NAKSEH—which means to step down. The famous Arab linguist Al Fairouzabadi discussed these expressions in his great encyclopedic dictionary (2). There are many new political expressions which appeared after World War 1. The Arabs had never used the word "revolution" before World War 1. They also hadn't used the word "war," as they had special names for battle. Instead, they used *yom*, which means day. For example, in the Holy Quran the expression *"Yom Hunaien"* (3) refers to the fierce battle of the prophet Mohammad with the non-believers at the dawn of Islam. Arabs have traditionally fought in the day light to avoid killing the innocent. Until 1920, Arab tribes never fought at night. War had traditions in the Arab culture. For example, they didn't kill sleeping persons (4), and they didn't build castles or fortifications. The idea of building a ditch around (El Madinat) the Holy City of the Prophet Mohammad and the first capital in Islam is a good example. The city was exposed to attacks from non-believers, and the Muslims were in a very poor defensive position. The idea to protect the city with a ditch appeared and was executed immediately by three thousand soldiers (warriors). It was not an Arab idea as Salman El Farsi (Persian), one of the Prophet mates, had suggested the idea of the ditch (5). The Arabs didn't build ditches or castles because of their dignity. They bravely fought and died for a cause in open air rather than being protected by a wall like the old Chinese Great Wall or a castle like the castles of the Crusaders. Most of the historical castles in Jordan were built by Crusader armies or prisoners from the Crusaders' Army. This subject is rather lengthy, so we will concentrate on the expressions and their relation to the causes of the Arab Spring in North Africa. It is worth mentioning here that the causes of the so-called Arab Spring are the same in the states of North Africa like Tunisia, Egypt, and Libya, and the Arab states in Asia like Yemen, Syria, and the rest of the Arab states who witnessed Arab Spring.

The Phrase "Arab Spring"

The phrase "The Arab Spring" was not coined by the Arabs. It is imported as it was previously used by the Western Media on several occasions. For example, the crisis which took place in Czechoslovakia was known as the Spring of 1968, describing the Warsaw pact joint maneuvers after the Dubcek government abandoned some reforms (6). The term (The Revolution of the Nile) later appeared in the Egyptian Press. Thus, this term is imported and may have been coined by the Western media referring to the shake off. In Libya the expression "7th February Revolution" is used (7).

The Approach of this Study

This study concentrates on the Content Analysis approach. We followed the events through the most prominent daily newspaper in Jordan (*Addstour*). This newspaper was our source for looking up and analyzing political, economic, and psychological terms that were used and reflected the causes of the so-called Arab Spring in Tunisia, Libya, and Egypt. The independent variables relate to the combinations of the causes of the Arab

Spring, like corruption, unemployment, and other elements. Although we aren't convinced that "Arab Spring" is the appropriate expression, we will use it because there are no other alternatives. A similar term in this regard is the "Middle East," which is not favored by most Arab intellectuals. They consider it colonial and reminiscent of the colonial powers, England and France, who coined this expression after the WW1 to refer to the area. Although Arabs criticized the expression, they never invented an alternative and it is still used in Arabic literature. It is worth mentioning here that most of the writers who have written about the Middle East are foreigners (See the names of the authors and books). (8)

The Phenomenon of the Name (El Boazeezi)

The new symbol of the change is the name "El Boazeezi." It is worth noting that a simple, single person was behind the so-called Arab Spring and we may argue that he exported the revolution to the Arab World. It should be recalled that revolution is traditionally exported by states rather than individuals. In El Boazeezi's case, a dead man exported the shake up to Egypt and the rest of the Arab World and the story started. He was the proverbial "straw that broke the camel's back."

The Roots of the El Boazeezi Phenomenon

The phenomenon of El Boazeezi appeared for the first time in the beginning of 2011. Mohammad El Boazeezi (26-year-old), who used to live in the small village of Seedi Abu Zaid, graduated from the university and did not find a job. He bought a small cargo of vegetables to sell. Municipal officials broke his cargo; when he went to the Municipality headquarter of Seedi Abu Zaidtocomplain, a policewoman who worked in the Municipality slapped him. He was humiliated. Since he was already fed up with the bad situation he lived in, he self-immolated over his cargo. The humiliation was the straw that broke the camel's back. The grass was dry and the fire blew up—society was ready for reform. The middle class in Tunisia were dissatisfied with the situation. There were many things to complain about, including poverty and the corruption of the government, which deprived the people of their wealth. The income of El Boazeezi, for instance, was $250 per month. People were frustrated for several reasons besides poverty; they had no right to practice their freedoms. For example, the freedom of religion was non-existent. Every citizen had to ask for permission before deciding at which mosque to pray. Women were not allowed to wear Islamic clothes. The middle class were deprived of the most essential things for their spiritual life. El Boazeezi paved the way for the revolt when he burnt himself on the 17th of December, 2010, and subsequently died after spending three weeks in the hospital. The pressure groups in Tunisia started to vocalize their discontent immediately. They were very thoughtful and expressed their point of view politely and peacefully. The government, however, was tough and used sharpshooters who killed civilians. After his death paved for the shakeup, protests started in Tunisia. There were other elements of society that contributed to the shake off as well, and they will be discussed later.

Imitation among Individuals – New Ways to Express Views and Frustrations

There was a very great reaction towards the events in Tunisia as the Arab World in North Africa and Asia was pleased. In Jordan, the people demonstrated to congratulate the Tunisian people by gathering in front the Tunisian Embassy. In the press, articles welcomed the developments in Tunisia, happy with the change. In Cairo, the same thing happened.

This is of secondary importance compared to the following phenomenon:

We may observe that the behavior of El Boazeezi, which led to the shake up, was exported to other Arab States and became a phenomenon among individuals who started to imitate and immolate themselves like El Boazeezi. This extended throughout the Arab states, and there were small cases of the influence which reached Europe. All these individuals who protested and burnt themselves proclaimed their mistreated by their governments. Thus, facing injustice or humiliation is the common factor between El Boazeezi and others who used the same method to express their dissatisfactions and frustrations. All the others who burnt themselves shared with El Boazeezi the following things:

1. Being humiliated by corrupted regimes.
2. Being unemployed and frustrated by the government.

The Reaction Abroad: Imitating the Burning

This method of protesting extended into the Arab World from Tunisia as individuals started to burn themselves.

- In Cairo, a man burnt himself in front of the Parliament on Monday 17th Jan 2011, protesting against poverty and the bad conditions in the country. The man was shouting "AMN EL DAWLA AMN ALDAWLA HAQI THIE JWA ELDAWLA" امن الدوله امن الدوله حقي ضايع جوا الدوله. This means, OH OH, THE SECURITY OF THE STATE; MY RIGHTS ARE VIOLATED INSIDE THE STATE. The man came from another city to Cairo. He faced a problem with the local administration that refused to give him what he ought to have for his restaurant. There was another case of a young man in his twenties who lived in Alexandria. His father accused him of being insane and he later died (9).

- In Algeria, there were eight persons who did the same thing later. They were in several cities. Not one of them died. The reason of these accidents was frustration with the government procedures. In Algeria, a man had an argument with a policeman after the policeman tried to give him a ticket. He stabbed him.

- In Mauritania, a rich businessman burnt himself protesting the treatment by the government against his family or tribe. On 23rd Jan 2011, the press announced that he had died. The government statements accused him of corruption.

- In Morocco and the Western desert, three men burnt themselves on 22nd Jan 2012.

- In the south of Saudi Arabia, a man burnt himself for unknown reasons on 22nd Jan 2011.

- In Sudan, a 25-year-old Sudanese worker originally from Darfur burnt himself in Um Darman in Sudan.

- Into Europe this amazing phenomenon extended—two accidents occurred there. In Romania, two persons burnt themselves on 19th Jan 2011, according to Media FAX Agency. The first was a 31-year-old who was suffering from poverty and couldn't provide food for his children. The second was a homeless man who was prevented from entering a shelter for the homeless people. Neither of them died. As of the 19th Jan, the number of people who have attempted to kill themselves was as follows: 8 people in Algeria, including one woman. One died. 6 people in Egypt. One died (10).

Notes

It seems that those who killed themselves were affected by the results of the case of El Boazeezi. As he motivated the people in his country to revolt, the people outside did the same thing to express their frustration.

Diagnosis of the Meaning of the Word Corruption

The diagnosis of the word "corruption," according to the people, is that the government understanding of the word "corruption" is corrupted. Thus, the point of view of the people is that corruption relates to governments rather than to the people's behavior. People blamed their governments, accusing them of corruption, lack of nationalism, and of burdening the people unfairly. They accused rulers of following a policy "Make your dog hungry, it will follow you" policy—but now they say, "Make your dog hungry, it will eat you"—the people will eat you. We want to highlight the role of the media and Internet tools, which accelerated the movement of the news from one place to another. *A combination of the word "corruption" and other words which caused the shake up:* The combination of several factors lead to this situation. The most important factors were unemployment, poverty, and corruption. There is one factor in our point of view that helped increase the frustration of the people—the collapse of the *image* of the governments and rulers and the *legitimacy* of the Arab rulers, especially those who were accused of a lack of patriotism. Their legitimacy was shaken as the Constitutional party had lost its legitimacy in Tunisia, and the people in Tunisia demanded new rulers, excluding anyone from the ex-party. The people disliked their leaders for many reasons like corruption and *lack of patriotism*. There was also a *lack of religious behavior* among some, like the Tunisian leader. The President of Tunisia wasn't liked by the people not because he was corrupt, but because he was accused of having secret relations with Israel before the Peace process started in Madrid in 1991. During the first years of the presidency, in 1988, the popular Palestinian leader Abu Jihad was killed in Tunisia by Israeli forces who attacked his residence. Accusations reached a high level in June 2011, suggesting that the Tunisian President was an Israeli agent.

The Importance of the Environment

The *importance of the environment* cannot be understated. The environment or dissent in Tunisia was conducive to change, as the government was looked upon by the people as corrupted and provocative to Islam. It was accused of building barriers between the people and their religion. After the collapse of the regime, the press published on the 22nd of January that the people were finally able to pray on Friday with freedom, as they were no longer afraid of the provocative procedures of the ex-regime. Women were finally able to wear their headscarves without any harassment by the Police. The environment of corruption and provocation of Islam by the ex-leaders, combined with miserable economic conditions, created the right environment for a shakeup. Thus, the social environment was ready for change at the start of the protests in Tunisia against the so-called "delicate dictatorship." Everyone believed that this regime was powerful and that they could not rid themselves of that fate.

Corruption of the Leaders

The corruption of the leaders in the eyes of the people in Tunisia and Egypt was a common factor. This corruption was further exposed by the media after the collapse of President Mubarak. Mubarak, who represented the old regime, reflected all kinds of corruption from the top along with his sons Jamal and Alaa. He was accused with his sons of taking bribes (the soft word "commission" is used here) (11). The Egyptian president was also accused of being bribed by Israel. This indicates that Mubarak was a very irresponsible and corrupted person. In Cairo, a psychologist said that Mubarak is a narcissist and that this was the result of him ruling for a long time. Mubarak had ruled for 30 years while Bin Ali the President of Tunisia had ruled for 24 years. Both of them enjoyed good relations with the Western states and Israel. This gave them confidence that they were politically immune, and they ignored the needs of the people, rather becoming businessmen or politicians surrounded by businessmen. This facilitated a weak, corrupted administration at all levels. This system is similar to that of other leaders like the Libyan President who ruled for 43 years; in Yemen, Ali Abdalla Salih ruled for 32 years. All of them shared the same qualities of corruption and ignoring their people's rights. This long period of rule contributed in killing the hope of the people in change or reform. The leaders in Egypt, Libya, and Yemen prepared their sons to inherit power (12).

A Class of Ruling Businessmen

There was a stratum or class of businessmen who ruled behind these miserable conditions. The leaders and their men created this class of Businessmen who had enormous wealth (13).

The priority in Egypt was similar to that in Tunisia—facing corruption as a common factor. This corruption was further exposed after the collapse of the President Mubarak. The businessmen had been ruling the country in the same manner they were running their businesses. Leaders had great confidence and they lost all motivation to reform, as they were very confident that they were protected and immune.

A Combination of Corruption and Humiliation

This important factor relates to the feeling of humiliation among all the Arabs and not only the youth. This frustration relates to the previous reasons and in specific the humiliation which the Arabs and Moslems felt after the campaign against Islam, which followed the events of September 11, 2001. The reaction of the people was signified in informal reactions that started in Tunisia and Egypt, and then the rest of the Arab states like Libya, Bahrain, and Yemen and to some extent in Jordan, Kuwait, UAE, and later in Syria. In the absence of the formal reactions from stronger Arab states like Egypt, new developments appeared in this vacuum as an informal reaction. Humiliation was accumulative and there were other reasons that contributed to increasing tension and frustrations like the economic difficulties which related to corrupted administration plus unemployment. The economy may in fact be the direct reason for all disruptive events that took place in the Arab World on several occasions before the so-called Arab Spring. For example, the shakeups in Jordan in 1989 and 1996 and in Egypt in 1977 and in Tunisia on several occasions were economic and didn't only relate to the political situation. Thus, disruption happened in two states in North Africa earlier and before the Arab Spring. There are other indirect reasons for the accumulative humiliation related to the campaign against terrorism that correlated terrorism with Islam before and after the invasion of Afghanistan. There were exaggerations in the media's campaign against Islam and against the so-called weapons of mass destruction in Iraq. With the new media methods and disinformation on the Internet, public opinion was combustible against the Western campaign against Islam and the occupation of Iraq and Afghanistan.

The Role of Homogeneous Feeling

These shakeups happened in Jordan before they happened in Tunisia or in the Arab World. They happened before the Arab Spring but were limited to one state and contained by the regime. The more recent protests happened in many states—they started with Tunisia and extended into to Egypt, Libya, Yemen, and then Syria. Perhaps the influence of satellite and new media methods assisted in creating a homogeneous feeling in the Arab world indicating real globalism. These media methods over the last ten years helped create one homogeneous feeling or opinion.

Evaluating the Point of View of Pressure Groups toward American Policy

The USA didn't necessarily back corruption in Egypt or Tunisia. Syria had strong bilateral relations with the USSR (and later Russia) and was still accused of corruption similar to that in Egypt and Tunisia. By comparison, Taiwan has good bilateral relations with the USA and is not corrupted. It has zero debt and the per Capita income is $37,000. The same is applicable to Japan and South Korea who have good bilateral relations with the USA. In the Arab world, there is a combination of causes that contribute to corruption. Nonetheless, the Arab people dislike the USA for its support for Israel. Leaders who are allies to the USA are far less popular than others. After the Arab Spring, the media in Egypt attacked new leaders who had had relations with the USA in the past. One clear example is the media attack on the current Egyptian president in the beginning of Jan 2013 because he said that he was working for NASA. He denied this, but the Egyptian Media showed two videos—one in which he made these statements, and a second in which he denied it.

In Libya, the current president Mustafa Abd El Jaleel wasn't inclined to deal with the USA or the west at the beginning, although he was obliged to do so when he needed them to get rid of the old regime.

The scandal of Wikileaks in the Arab world (regarding the USA role) shocked the American and some Arab rulers' image and made it worse than it was.

The Shakeup of the Pressure Groups in North Africa

By the beginning of 2011, for the first time in recent Arab history, pressure groups started the so-called Arab Spring in Tunisia. The pressure groups in the Arab world moved to overthrow old regimes. Traditionally, these groups usually pressured governments to change; however, this time they changed the rulers and the phenomenon extended from Tunisia to Egypt, then Yemen, Bahrain, and Libya. The Arabs in Africa make up 72% of the population of the Arab world (two-thirds of these Arabs are in North Africa).

Pressure Groups

"Pressure Groups" in Political Science are different from political parties. They don't want to rule, they don't have a cadre and employees, and they don't receive foreign support from the outside (while political parties do want to rule, do have cadres, and do receive foreign support). In Egypt and Tunisia these pressure Groups appeared quickly to express their frustrations against:

> Humiliation
>
> Corruption
>
> Unemployment

The Background and Methods of Participants

The participants of this extraordinaty movement are ordinary people. They are pressure groups, not political parties.

The Methods of these pressure Groups were more peaceful than the governments.

These people belonged to the middle class and started their protest movement politely and continued in this way despite being ordinary people. They are pressure groups, not politicians. After the government used tough procedures by using thugs and sharpshooters to kill civilians, the Pressure Groups escalated their demands. This immoral behavior was done by the Egyptian, Libyan, and Tunisian governments. The people were not afraid anymore. This corresponds with the Arab proverb that says that the drowned person is not afraid of getting wet.

The people who are protesting in Egypt are two-thirds of the population of Egypt and 90% of them are unemployed, according to the press. There was a call for one million demonstrators in Egypt on 29th Jan 2012.

The Egyptian Army consists of 468,000 members; it is the tenth largest army in the world. Furthermore, the number of the security forces is approximately 1,400,000. But here we observe the role of unemployment, which is clearly one of the real factors in the uprising or shakeup. People may bear everything like corruption, lack of nationalism, and humiliation if they have jobs and monthly income. For example, we may observe that people in Iraq during the era of Sadam Hussein did not have democracy, but they had security and jobs. Now the Iraqis are longing for the days of Sadam when they had security and effective services. Ultimately, unrest is a matter of priorities.

The Pressure Groups Use Names and Titles

In Egypt, pressure groups are as follows: the Youth in the El Tahreer circle (Square) are called The Coalition Youth of the Revolution (Shabab Etaaluf El Thawra). There is a confederation of the Youth of April movement and the Coalition of the Revolution Youth who led the uprising on 25th January. It is observable that this direction is similar to that of Tunisia where they choose the names of these pressure groups who changed the regimes. There is another Movement whose name is The Popular Democratic Movement, which states in its manifesto that it doesn't want a new dictator.

In Egypt and Libya, the leaders prepared their sons to replace them.

In Libya, the Transitional National Council was founded in Benghazi by the revolutionaries. This is the political power of opponents in Libya. France was the first to recognize this council on Sunday the 6th of March 2011.

In Libya, both sides of the leaders and the pressure groups used violence. There was an international intervention in Libya, a political intervention by the UN and the Arab League, and a military intervention by NATO.

The Role of the Absence of the Formal Reaction

In the absence of any formal reaction from the Arab leaders, informal reaction appeared from the Arab People. This reaction was strong and continuous— pressure groups demanded reform at the beginning, but later they demanded more—the removal of the leaders. When the accident of El Boazeezi succeeded in igniting the shakeup in Tunisia, the young generation was affected by the results of the events. After they had lost hope for a bright future and with the combination of all the reasons which were mentioned earlier, they began to organize their protests.

This happened in Tunisia, Egypt, and Libya. The events in Egypt began similarly to those in Tunisia—the middle class was frustrated; there was a lot of corruption. The pressure groups started the shakeup politely and peacefully in Tunisia and Egypt, demanding change. Day after day, the people became more frustrated, and hatred increased toward the rulers. No one wanted to confess that there was a very great deal of hostility and anger. We have noted that this sentiment was an accumulation of causes, some of them direct and strong but others indirect. For example, some years ago the Arabs suffered (and still do) from the humiliation of the American occupation of Iraq. Although the people don't openly talk about their opinions, they express them in their private meetings. It had been predicted that these uprisings could have happened before if there had been backing for the people to start protesting. Even though there was no encouragement from the outside, they had started to demonstrate. Demonstrations came to the streets in these states whose governments were allies to USA, like Tunisia or Egypt. They reached Yemen and Algeria. There have been continuous demonstrations. What was new is that people insisted on their demands. People were following up and this was a new phenomenon.

The developments in Egypt indicated that the pressure groups were effective. In their methods, these pressure groups behaved politely and in a very high standard of responsibility. The governments in most of these states were not polite or responsible. There were thugs who appeared and killed protestors in Egypt, Tunisia, and Libya.

In Egypt and Tunisia, people hate the symbols of the old regimes of Mubarak and Zain El Abdeen. In Libya, the situation deteriorated after demonstrators demanded the removal of the President, and after the regime's brutal response.

In Libya people moved against the President. The results of the events encouraged the young generations that there was hope in putting pressure on their leaders. All the leaders in Tunisia, Egypt, and Libya had military backgrounds and came from the army or security forces. In the past, the army used to lead the change. In the fifties, change in the Arab world came from officers backed by Western powers, as in Egypt in 1952. Later, the ruling officers in Egypt backed the revolution in Iraq on 14 July 1958, in Yemen in 1961, in Iraq in 1963, and in Libya in 1969. Now the protests were against the leaders, some of whom had military backgrounds. The shakeup—civilian pressure—is escalating every few minutes in the Arab World. The file is open as long as the underlying causes remain.

Notes

1. Ali, Ahmed, *Al–Quran, A Contemporary Translation*. Karachi Akashi Publishing, 1985.

2. Al Fairouzabadi, Migd Eldeen Mohamad bin Yaqoub, El Qamous El Moheet, 2nd edition (Beirut; Moassat Elresaleh) 1987, pp. 178, 746.

3. The Holy Quran (Surra 9 in the Holy Quran).

4. The secret instructions of John Bajot Glubb, the leader of the Jordanian Arab Legion to the British Officers in Jordan. Glubb served in Jordan and Iraq during the period 1921–1956. He was in the Army all the time and spent time in the desert among the Bedouins. Dr Saad Abudayeh reviewed his papers in Saint Antony College, The Middle East Centre in Oxford, UK, and wrote his book *The Lord of Desert*. All these instructions are in *The Lord of Desert* (Amman: Dar El Basheer) 2006, pp. 143-153.

5. Hassan, Ibrahim Hassan, *The History of Islam; Political, Religious, Cultural, and Social* 7th edition (Beirut; Dar El Andalus), 1964.

6. K. J. Holsti, *International Politics – A framework for analysis* (New Jersey: Prentice Hall 1972, pp. 283-284).

7. *Addastour* Jordanian Daily Newspaper. We followed the news in this paper since the beginning of January 2011. See specifically the events from 18 Jan 2011 until 8 Feb 2011.

8. The books about the Middle East are: Armagani, yaha *Middle East Past and Present* (New Jersey: Prentice Hall, 1980), p. 1; Kavunadus, Tomas, *The Middle East* (Bronxville Cambridge Book Co., 1968, p. 1; Lenczowski, George, *The Middle East in the World Affairs* (Ithaca and London Cornell University Press, 1979), p. 8; Harkavy, Robert, Strategic Accesses Bases, and Arms Transfers: The Major Powers' Evolving Geopolitical Competition in the Middle East (New York: Pergamum Press, 1979), p. 17; J. K. Banarji, *The Middle East in World Politics* (Calcutta, The World Press Private Ltd, 1960), pp. 1-2.

9. *Addastour*, 18 Jan 2011.

10. Ibid, and 8 March 2012.

11. Haikal, Mohammad Hasneen, *Mubarak Wa Zamanuh: Matha Jara fee Masr Wa howlaha* (Cairo: Shorouq, 2012), pp. 403-420. The title of this book may be translated: *The Time of Mubarak the President of Egypt: What Happened in Egypt and the Surrounding Area*. The writer discusses corruption,

and claims that the presidency informally received around 800 million EP from the Suez Canal revenues annually.

12. Haikal, Mohammad Hasneen, *Ma baaed Mubarak Wa Zamanuh* (Cairo: Shorouq, 2012), pp. 83-94, 117-136. The title of this book is: *Egypt to Where*. The writer discusses the subject of inheritance of the presidency between Mubarak the President and his son.

13. El Minyawi, Ramzi, *Rajul min Jahanam* (Allepo: Darelketab, 2012), pp. 138-142. The title of the book in English is *A Man from Hell*. The writer discusses the corruption of the ex-Libyan president; El Quwayeeri, Omar Hassan, That El Rejal, "Eye witnesses and events" (Benghazi: Libya Elghad CO, 2012). This book discusses the events, accidents, and the situation during the time of the ex-President of Libya. He called the revolution the REVOULTION OF 17 FEBURUARY. This book is more rational than the other book about the Libyan president by El Minyawi, Ramzi, *Rajul min Jahanam*.

CHAPTER 2

The Arab Spring and Pressure Groups

For the first time in the recent history, "the pressure groups" in the Arab world moved to overthrow current regimes. Usually, these groups make change by influencing governments and convincing them to change their decisions. This phenomenon extended initially from Tunisia to Egypt and then spread out to Yemen, Bahrain, and Libya. Mainly, the battlefield was situated in the Middle East and in North Africa. It is worth mentioning that 72 percent of the area of the Arab world is in Africa. I assume in my study that the "pressure groups" in the region at this time are in the process of change. "Pressure groups" are concentrating on putting pressure on governments. They are different from political parties in that they do not want to rule, and they do not have candidates in elections in contrast to political parties. I will use both historical and analytic approaches to describe this issue. I will depend on Jordanian media sources, mainly the daily newspaper *Ad-Dustour*.

The Tunisian Young Man, El Bouazizi

In the beginning of 2011 "pressure groups" started the "Arab Spring" in Tunisia. The story started on the 17th of December 2010, when a young man, 23-year-old Muhammad Al Bouazizi, set himself on fire in front of a government building. His tragedy became a catalyst for changes in Tunisia and in the Middle East. It was an example of humiliation to which the citizens in the Middle East are often exposed. The Tunisian young man El Bouazizi is an example of the typical Arab youth. He could not find a job and started to work as a street vendor selling vegetables. His monthly income was about 250 USD. The municipality seized his goods and car. El Bouazizi was humiliated when he attempted to complain to restore his rights—a female police officer slapped him in the face. As a result of all the humiliation, the young man set himself on fire, and he died two weeks later. His death paved the way for revolt.

Serious social tensions rose in Tunisia and the climate for change became ripe. Al Bouazizi's death was "the straw that broke the camel's back." The middle class has been dissatisfied with the situation. Unemployment, poverty, and corruption have affected Tunisia.

In Tunisia, the government has never been popular and officials have never taken into consideration people's opinions. Representatives of the ex-ruling establishment felt safe, immune from social influence. The official position of the state was based on strong bilateral relationships with USA and France.

Convenient Space for Revolution

The safety for revolution they had hoped for proved to be illusory because that was already created and "pressure groups" in Tunisia were ready. Tunisians were afraid of actions performed by the ex-regime, which was accused by the people not only of corruption and unemployment, but also of depriving them of their rights to worship. Women were prevented from entering public institutions wearing "hijab." Moreover, many of them wearing "hijab" could not be employed by government institutions. Men were also frustrated about the aforementioned issues.

The Methods of Expression of the People's Will

All "pressure groups" in the region started to influence public opinion in a very balanced way, demanding the peaceful revolt. Usually, they concentrated on the government. They do not expect to be allowed to share power and their goals differ from those of political parties, who are trying to gain adequate representation in the government to be more influential.

What Are the Real Reasons and Results of the Political Developments in the Middle East?

There is no doubt that U.S. policy has helped the situation to reach this level of surprise. The USA and Europe have weakened the Arabs. Because of their policies, powerful Arab states like Egypt and Iraq are set apart from Arab regional activities. Egypt has turned out to be, in the last thirty years, a "small state" of decreasing importance, and Iraq, occupied by the U.S. from 2003 to 2011, became a nation of exclusion.

The Informal Reaction in the Arab World

In the absence of formal reactions from the Arab states, informal reactions from the Arab people appeared. These actions were strong and continuous. In this case, the following important phenomena was observed: spontaneous behavior of people, described as informal reactions that started first in Tunisia, later in Egypt, and then in the rest of the Arab states, like Libya, Bahrain, or Yemen, and to some extent in Jordan. Other countries like Kuwait, the UAE, and Syria were also infected with this phenomenon.

A Completely New Social Issue Related to Two Factors:

1) The strong humiliation, frustration, and difficulties which Arab and Muslims citizens have been exposed to after 2001. The developments that followed these events and the accusations against Islam and Arabs created frustration in hearts of many Muslims and Arabs, which was compounded by the agony of the Palestinians and Iraqis under occupation. All these events and the new shape of Western foreign policy, accompanied by media campaigns filled with hate against the Arabs, increased tensions. There are other reasons that contributed to the existing tension and frustration level in Arab societies, like economic difficulties related to corrupted administrations as well as the Israeli position in the peace process.

2) The absence of a formal reaction. There were no official reactions presented by the Arab and Muslim governments towards this humiliation. A lack of reaction paved the way to the people's informal reaction. No one predicted it. It appeared suddenly and in an unexpected way. It was directed against the allies of the USA and the Western states.

Iran as a New Player in the Middle East

The second thing that has suddenly appeared in the region is reaction by Iran, who at first cooperated with USA and later started to weaken American influence in the region. Since 1982, Iran has succeeded in creating its strong position in Lebanon, in a country that threatens Israel, the inviolable ally of the USA.

The Phenomenon of "Gangsters"

The outcome of the developments in Egypt was positive for the "pressure groups." They were very effective thanks to the methods used. They behaved in a very balanced and smart way, "politely" and with a very high standard of responsibility. In contrast to them, representatives of the government, police, and military forces in Egypt showed a lack of responsibility. They were acting like "gangsters" who committed violent actions towards protestors. Military, police officers, and security forces were responsible for killing demonstrators in Libya, Tunisia, and Egypt. In some countries like

Bahrain, police forces were extremely violent. Even in Jordan (on the 18th February 2011), the demonstrators were exposed to violent attacks performed by "unidentified perpetrators." Fourteen of them were arrested by security forces. Due to this situation, Jordanian authorities decided to increase future levels of protection for demonstrators.

The "follow-up" phenomenon. Tunisian clashes inspired protests in several other Arab countries, as well as in some non-Arab countries. "Arab Spring" was created by this "follow-up" phenomenon. In Egypt, "pressure groups" followed up the process initiated in Tunisia. Protesters stepped up pressure on Hosni Mubarak. The president at a certain moment moved outside Cairo and was hiding in Sharm El Sheikh. That was frustrating for Egyptians, as well as the fact that according to the press and Internet media, the wealth of his family was estimated at 160 Billion USD. It was also discovered that some of the Suez Canal profits went to Mubarak's family and to army officials. People still look for change and their demands are unfulfilled. Additionally, relations between the army and people exposed tensions. The Tunisian people succeeded to continue pressure and succeeded in removing the prime, Minister El Ghounshi, after they had already overthrown the president, Zine Al-Abidine Ben Ali, who fled his country after weeks of mass protests. In Egypt and Tunisia, people hate symbols of the old regimes of the ex-presidents, but there are many differences between both nations.

Developments in Libya

The Mercenaries in Libya New Phenomenon

In Libya, people moved against the president, Muammar Gaddafi (Ghathafi, Al Gathafi), who appeared to be a brutal "gangster." He and his sons used jet fighters and heavy weapons against protestors. But the reaction of people was stronger in unity and they stood firmly against him. As a result of the Libyan civil war a new leader emerged, the Minister of Justice, Mr. Mustafa Abd El Jaleel.

In the beginning he did not want assistance from foreigners. He appeared on TV and threatened foreign forces involved in the Libya conflict. He promised that they would face a force stronger than the mercenaries. This reaction came shortly after the statement by the American U.S. Secretary of State, Hilary Clinton, who said that she had contacted the group of opponents in the Eastern part of Libya. The mercenaries in Libya were brought in from African states by planes. Some of them came from Kenya. The UN Security Council announced a resolution on 26ᵗʰ February 2011 which did not prevent planes from flying over Libya as had happened in Iraq. This approach helped mercenaries to be transferred to Libya from the neighboring states. Ghathafi's weakness was lack of a loyal army because he was afraid that the national military forces might try to organize a *coup d'état* against him. As a result, he used mercenaries; despite their involvement, he was killed.

In Bahrain, people are still demonstrating even after cabinet changes in the government introduced by the king. They are demanding a transition to a "constitutional monarchy." I think they will continue protesting for their "legitimate demands." In Yemen, the current situation is very serious. Many innocent people have lost their lives as a result of numerous protests. People still keep the peaceful trend, but the situation may escalate. The GGC is constantly involved in new initiatives related to Yemen, but it is difficult to forecast how advanced the transition of power will be in this country. An additional factor that makes this situation more complicated is the uncompromising behavior of President Ali Abdullah Saleh towards his own people. According to the security forces, the president is going to choose a peaceful transition of power. Unfortunately, it takes time because he and his relatives fully control Yemen. All main positions in the country are headed by his relatives:

1) his son Ahmad is the Head of the Republican Guards,
2) his nephew Yehia Mohammad is the Head of the Central Security,
3) his nephew Tariq Mohammad is the Head of Private Guards,
4) his nephew Ammar Mohammad is the Deputy of National Security,
5) his half-brother Ali Mohsen Saleh El Ahmar holds position of the Head of the First Regiment,
6) his nephew Tawfeeq Saleh Abdalla the Head of Air Forces.

There are also other high rank positions (i.e., Deputy of the Prime Minister, ministers, governors, mayors, directors of national companies representing tobacco and oil industry, ambassadors, deputies of ministers and several Army leaders) ruled by people representing his tribe.

Jordanian Opponents Outside Jordan and "Electronic Opposition"

On the 24th of July 2011, newspaper *Ad-Dustour* announced that there were Jordanian opponents outside Jordan, living in England, the USA, Australia, and Western Europe. Maher Abu Tair wrote that "in the past it was said that Jordan is the only Arab State who has no "outside opponents" of the government." As we know from the 1960s and 1970s, Jordanian opposition situated outside Jordan decided to return to Jordan after being issuing a special public pardon by the king. According to M. Abu Tair, "opponents nowadays use the Internet to express their views and opinions. Inside Jordan there are also other opponents, well organized, who represent political parties and these people know what they want." Their actions should be taken under consideration by government. These opponents should not be ignored. What will the future of the opposition of this kind be? In my opinion, in countries like Jordan and Egypt, such movements growing through the Internet can be more efficient than in Syria, Yemen, or Saudi Arabia. Oppositionists from outside and inside Jordan are using all possible methods available to make their influence on government stronger. The opposition outside Jordan is free and able to attack without constraint. Their actions are directed towards many key officials gathered around the king. Criticizing the royal family is a new phenomenon in Jordan. Several analysts are saying that historically, Jordanians do not cross certain lines of criticism but these days, some of the opponents "cross the traditional borders." There are many reasons this situation was strengthened by "Arab Spring." Traditionally, Jordanians respect the Hashemite and in my opinion, there is still existing support among opponents towards the monarchy.

Fighting corruption is a priority in Jordan that requires a genuine and serious approach. In Jordan, people demand stronger enforcement in the fight against corruption. There are several important issues that have been submitted to the Anti-Corruption Commission. According to the Jordanian media, one of them is a case related to the development project "Sakn Kareem" ("generous housing") where some discrepancy were recorded. The second issue is called "Mawarid" and is related to land sales. The third was connected to the project concerning a "Casino." Actually, all of them are under investigation. In my point of view, if these cases are not treated with transparency and firmness, in the future Jordan may expect more tensions. H.M. King Abdullah II has the opportunity to take the initiative and begin a new era in Jordan by creating efficient political and economical reforms that will be positively received by Jordanians. There is a need to perform these reforms immediately. Currently, the most important issue in Jordan is finding and keeping professional and well-qualified representatives of the nation in government.

"Pressure Group" Activity in Jordan

The Arab world is in a transition period. The role of "pressure groups" is still increasing. In Jordan, "pressure groups" started their activity in January 2011, earlier than similar groups operating in Tunisia. By then, no one anticipated how they would develop, how dangerous and influential they would be, and in what ways they would criticize the representatives of the government or how they would organize protests. In Jordan, people had taken to the streets to demand action on rising prices, high unemployment, and political reforms. On Sunday, January 16, 2011, the government announced a reduction of prices on several food products like sugar, yogurt, and imported meat. Unfortunately, people were not satisfied with it because in their opinions nothing has changed. On the 22nd January 2011, an increase of monthly salaries of 20 JD (28 USD) was officially announced. Before the collapse of the Tunisian government, the Jordanian government reduced the prices of fuel, which it had raised just two weeks earlier. Protesters were demanding the resignation of Prime Minister Samir Rifai. Some demonstrations took place in Amman and outside the capital. People were calling for more efficient political, legal, and economical actions.

Jordan, Egypt, Tunisia, and Yemen share common problems in the Middle East, among them poverty and unemployment. At the same time, many businessmen and representatives of the ruling class are very skeptical about introducing new reforms. This is the reason why disappointment reached its peak in Egypt, Tunisia, and Libya. In Jordan, people were complaining mostly about unemployment, the increase of prices, and to some extent about corruption. As a result of this process, some countries witnessed increased movement by "pressure groups," i.e., in Bahrain or Libya, citizens not only complain of poverty but suffer from lack of freedom. In Jordan, after 25th March 2011, the protests became a higher risk and the number of critics increased. H. M. Abdullah II was stable in his democratization approach. He was personally involved in constitutional reforms. Together with the queen, they visited residents of cities and villages in far areas of Jordan, and they financially supported them. In March 2011 a new prime minister, Mr. Marouf Al Bakhit, was appointed. His government assisted poor people living in remote regions of Jordan in housing and medical treatment. Despite of these activities, people still expect further changes and more initiatives for them and the country. The situation still requires active reforms and procedures to improve the situation in Jordan.

The Jordanian "March 24th Group"

There are two main demands of the society in Jordan: increasing the standard of living and fighting against corruption. Such ideas like closing the Embassy of Israel in Amman or immediately changing the electoral system in Jordan are more slogans than real demands. In my opinion, many things should be ignored by Jordanians if the government is serious about enacting reforms.

On 25th March 2011, again tensions flared in Jordan. Protesters in Amman were demanding the resignation of Prime Minister Marouf Al-Bakhit, reforms to parliament, and more efficient action against corruption. The number of NGOs and representatives of Unions who joined the "March 24th Group" movement increased. The Islamic Action Front did not participate in this demonstration. In my opinion, the Islamic movement shared the view that these people were from different backgrounds and they would not influence the current situation. According to many Jordanian media, "it was a serious mistake to accept the situation in which 'unidentified perpetrators' attacked demonstrators on 25th March 2011." This has happened for the second time in a short period of time. As a result of these protests, one person died and many people were injured, among them some police officers. After that event, a press release announced that reforms would continued and that all people involved in illegal practices would stand trial.

A New Approach Towards Crisis

In the Gulf states like Oman, financial concerns preoccupied the opposition. Omani people were not against the Head of State. They demanded employment and strong anti-corruption actions. There were two strikes, one in Muscat and second in Sahar. One person was killed during protests. As a result of this death, the police director and 13 ministers were dismissed. Many new procedures have been introduced since protests started in February 2011. To restore the previous situation, thousands of jobs were created and pensions were increased. On 10th March 2011, the Gulf Council Cooperation (GCC) decided to form a trust of $20 Billion USD to assist Bahrain and Oman. A few days later, on 13th March 2011, a special committee to reform constitution was formed and many of the PMs were replaced.

In Bahrain, according to *Al Wast* and *Ad-Dustour* newspapers (articles published on 7th March 2011), the only response of the government to the people's demands was a declaration to create thousands of new jobs and continue the dialogue with society. As Robert Fisk reported in the *Independent* and *Ad-Dustour* newspapers (dated 8th March 2011), the "situation in Bahrain is far from being stable. Financial procedures introduced by government were not sufficient." Additionally, new protests against naturalized citizens of Bahrain appeared. Criticism against the government increased and opponents continued their demands to form a new constitution.

In Saudi Arabia, similar trends were observed. "The minimum salaries rate" was introduced, as well as special initiatives towards unemployment and in the housing sector. Additionally, an Anti-Corruption Department was established.

Self-immolation

The way of protesting by self-immolation extended from Tunisia to other Arab countries, first to Egypt, where on Monday, 17th January 2011, in Cairo in front of the Parliament, a man set fire to himself protesting against poverty and the bad conditions in the country. Then in Algeria, eight people did the same thing protesting against government decisions. Finally in Mauritania, a rich businessman died on 23rd January 2011 as a result of self-immolation.

The Palestinian Issue and the Arab Spring

In my opinion, during "Arab Spring" it was observed that "pressure groups" also put Palestinian issues on their agenda. Numerous demonstrations related to this issue took place in the region (also in Jordan). Palestinian "pressure groups" in Jordan supported the rights of Palestinians to return to their homeland. The first demonstration took place on Friday 13th May 2011 in the downtown area of Amman. The second took place in the Jordan Valley. In the newspaper *Ad-Dustour*, published on the 14th May 2011, Yassir Zaatreh mentioned that "these Palestinian rallies and marches has attracted the attention in region, because also in Egypt similar marches were organized."

Arab Spring "Paved the Way for Strikes"

In Jordan, "Arab Spring" paved the way to mass protests and several strikes.

According to the announcement of Jordanian Ministry of Political Development, the total number of demonstrations in 2011 reached more than 3,000. A few strikes were noted and some of them were staged by medical doctors. The Jordanian government tried to convince society that the current economic crisis and problems with the gas supply from Egypt were having a negative impact on the national financial budget. People were expecting quick improvement concerning possible joining GCC by Jordan.

The Idea to Initiate "Dialogue" Again

In Bahrain, the King asked speaker of the Upper House to start a "dialogue" with people. The beginning of talks was expected in July 2011. A more advanced approach was adopted in Jordan. In March 2011, H.M. Abdullah II established National Dialogue Committee and in April 2011 he announced constitution reforms, which would be performed by Royal Committee to Amend the Constitution. In July 2011, King Abdullah II issued decree resulting reconstruction of the government.

In Yemen, there was trend to return to talks and continue the dialogue. The USA and Europe encouraged this process. Unfortunately, this idea failed.

In Syria, talks about dialogue started with the nation and representatives of Baath Party. According to Article 8 of the Constitution, the Baath Party is a ruling party in the state. It is guaranteed 126 out of 250 seats in parliament. The opposition is divided and not prepared to act in cooperation with various groups of protesters. In a conference that was held by the opponents of Syria in Turkey on 1st June 2011 the Muslim Brotherhood representatives talked about "dialogue," but they put many conditions that are difficult or impossible to accept by representatives of Syrian authorities (like official state apology or release of prisoners). There are many indicators why the Western media have not received Syrian actions with positive response. I wish to underline importance of the fact that reality in Syria is far different as the situation in Yemen, Tunisia, Jordan, or Bahrain. The Western community is divided and there is no clear and common attitude towards government in Damascus. China and Russia are against any military involvement and sanctions against this country. Additionally, there are close relations between Damascus and Teheran.

In Egypt, it was difficult to conduct a peaceful dialogue over crucial national issues. Many institutions and informal groups were involved in the process of political changes. Among them were youth groups like "the Youth of April" movement and the "Coalition of the Revolution Youth" actively engaged in mass protests. They were against formal dialogue with representatives of the "old regime," especially with ruling military council. Oppositionists were focused on political issues and their expectations were related to democratization of the country without military involvement.

The "dialogue"

The "dialogue" in the Middle East and North Africa will continue, but I am not sure if it will have positive and peaceful results like it did in Tunisia. People still desire reforms. In Egypt, Libya, and Tunisia, they succeeded to overthrow their leaders, but the future of democratic changes in spite of their success is not certain. In Yemen there has been great resistance from the leadership to give up the power. In these circumstances, it is difficult for protesters to push their demands as conflicts escalates. As a result of escalation of this conflict was bomb attack on Yemeni president that took place on Friday, 3rd June 2011. At the end of 2011, demonstrators were concentrated on removing their leader. I still hope that the president will take into consideration the opinion of the nation, and he will decide to resign in order to initiate process of changes.

The "Fatwa"

The "Fatwa" as another new phenomenon in the "Arab Spring." The Fatwa is religious instrument that was in use in the past and during this year's "Arab Spring." In Yemen, Sheikh Abdelmajeed Aziz Al-Zindani, a preacher and influential politician, co-founder of the Muslim Brotherhood in Yemen, stated that he "approves changes related to the constitution and the law, conducted in a manner that protects the country from strife." In his opinion, "it is not permitted to go out and protest against the authority that has been given the allegiance of the people except in the instances where they cannot govern the country due to illness or old age." Al-Zindani added that peaceful demonstrations are not against the religion. The International Council of the Muslim Scientists headed by Yousef Gharthawi (Egyptian living in Qatar) made a statement that demands of the Yemeni people are righteous. Their actions were described as legal voice for prompt changes that was in accordance with principles of Islam.

On the other hand, Abd al-Aziz al-Ashaikh, scholar and Grand Mufti of Saudi Arabia, declared on 6th March 2011 that "any form of demonstration in the country is against religion and the prophet Mohammad."

In Jordan, in March 2011, the Islamic Action Front had announced another "Fatwa" that permitted demonstrations in the country. But few days later, on the 10th March 2011, religious leaders declared reforms as a form of "dialogue without demonstration."

In Kuwait, on 10th March 2011, General Secretary of the Islamic Movement Mr. Badr El Shabeeb declared that "demonstrations are not a part of religious practices and should not be an issue related to 'Fatwa.'" B. El-Shabeeb added that "Muslims also have the right to extend their opinions and they should be heard by their rulers."

Conclusions and Remarks

Developments in the Middle East and North Africa reflect the "pressure of groups" that have hanged the future of the Arab world. In my opinion new developments were observed in the region since "Arab Spring" started:

1) **"Fatwa"** announced by the religious leaders to give legitimacy to the demonstrations.

2) The phenomenon of **"electronical opposition"** movements (opponents using internet to express their views)—effective in Egypt and Tunisia and to some extent in Jordan.

3) The idea of giving certain names to **Fridays** demonstrations.

4) **Self-immolation** as a symbol against regime (as it happened in Tunisia). Such drastic actions were repeated also in Europe and in the USA (on Thursday 10th November 2011, when a young man burned himself to death in protest). The "Occupy Wall Street" movement in the U.S. repeated some of the Egyptian "experiments" that took place in Tahrir Square in Cairo (Medan El Tahreer).

5) The **"idea of dialogue"** between the government and the opponents and the appearance of the "Transitional Councils" which became temporary governments (this has happened in Libya but failed in Syria).

6) Using the Arab League support to give legitimacy to temporary governments (called **"Councils"**); this was successful in Libya, but it failed in Syria.

7) The appearance of **"gangsters"**—"representatives of terror without names," groups of unidentified individuals involved in threatening

protesters to secure position of the current establishment ("regime establishment"). Their role is the same in many countries in the region, but their names are different, i.e. in Syria they are called "**Shabeeha**" and in Egypt "**Baltagi**."

8) Increasing position and political involvement of "**pressure groups**" and their representatives. In general, "pressure groups" succeeded to overthrow leaders in several countries like Tunisia, Egypt, and Libya during first months of their activity. In Tunisia the head of the state left to Saudi Arabia. In Egypt H. Mubarak left the capital to Sharm El Sheikh. Today he and his sons are on trial, and they face charges of corruption and unlawful killing. Libya's head of state was brutally killed. In Yemen it is a matter of time to apply the GCC initiative. In Bahrain the crisis continues. In Syria the government accepted the mediation and involvement of the Arab League. Syria survived the great Western pressure with the assistance of China and Russia who helped this country to avoid UN Security Council involvement in Syrian internal affairs.

9) Increase of political activity of some of the countries in the region. Involvement of Turkey in Syria crisis and Qatar's activity in Libya were unexpected. Analysts see unprecedented role of **Qatari TV** "Al Jazeera" in the "Arab Spring" revolutions.

10) "**Stability of kingdoms**." It is not coincidental that several countries were not seriously affected by the "Arab Spring." The stability of Gulf kingdoms is the result of their financial situation, which is in close relation to their revenues from the petroleum industry. Stability in Morocco and particularly in Jordan is a clear result of reforms that were initiated in the past. It is worth mentioning that another factor for stability in Jordan is active financial involvement of Saudi Arabia. In 2011, Saudi Arabia granted Jordan $1 Billion USD. In my opinion all problems in the Arab world are related to the economy, unemployment, and corruption. In rich states like Saudi Arabia, the king is coping with problems by granting salaries and finding jobs for the youth.

I share the view that there were many reasons for protests in the region during "**Arab Spring**." There are common factors among them, like corruption, unemployment, and lack of freedom. The way, in which Arab governments deal with these issues is different. Protesters are facing different approaches. I think that the approach of the Jordanian authorities is very rational one.

Chapter 3

The Ongoing Challenge of Pressure Groups in the Events of the Middle East – The Post Tunisian Era

Abstract

For the first time in the history of the world, in the beginning of 2011 a novel phenomenon emerged in the Arab world. The phenomenon concerns events that spread out in the area covering Egypt, Tunisia, Bahrain, Yemen, and several other countries like Algeria, for instance. I assume that pressure groups, not political parties, are behind the events. Let me mention that the pressure groups in Political Science differ from parties. Pressure groups do not want to rule; they do not have cadres and employees, and do not receive foreign support from outside. The political parties instead want to rule, have cadres, and receive foreign support. In my follow up of the events unfolding since January 2011, I depended on one of the Jordanian newspapers: *Addustour*.[1]

I found the assumption that the pressure groups in the Arab World are more important than political parties, as they are at the rear of most events, among which the so-called "Arab Spring" has a relevant place. They are still active and the reasons for their protest are still there too.

The Pressure Groups, Parties, Demonstrations, Gangsters, and the Arab Springs

Suddenly for the first time in the history, a novel phenomenon emerged in the Arab world. This phenomenon concerns events that spread out in the area covering the area in Egypt and Tunisia these. It is the Pressure Groups that emerged soon on the scene to express the frustrations of the people against humiliation in the first place. The young Tunisian, El Boazeezi ,who triggered the string of events in the Middle East was humiliated on 17 December 2010, when he was slapped in the face by female police officer. It all started like this. El Boazezzi was selling groceries from his carriage. The municipality broke the carriage to prevent him from selling in the streets. He went to the Municipality to complain. In return a female police officer slapped him. He felt humiliated. As he was already fed up with his precarious living conditions, he set himself on fire in protest. That was the straw that broke the camel's back. We may metaphorically say the grass was al-

ready dry and the fire extended quickly. The circumstances were ripe for reforms. It is the old story of prophets who look for the right background for
their preaches. The middle class in Tunisia were highly dissatisfied. They
had many things to complain about: first the general poverty, then the corruption of the government who deprived the people from their wealth. The
income of El Boazeezi was $250 every month. There are several reasons for
the people to complain; for example, the people did not have the right to
practice their religion. Every citizen had to ask for and get prior permission
where to pray, in which mosque. Girls were not allowed to wear the Islamic
clothes. The middle class was deprived of basic necessities to make their
living. After three weeks in hospital, El Boazeezi died (in the beginning of
2011). He paved the way for the revolt that was soon to erupt. The pressure
groups in Tunisia started to express their discontent immediately. They
were very thoughtful and expressed their point of view politely and peacefully. The government was tough and used sharpshooters killing dozens of
civilians.[2]

The Developments in Egypt a New Role of the Pressure Groups in the Arab World and the Weakness of the Administration Departments

The developments that took place subsequently in Egypt, Tunisia, and Jordan were not counted for by any of the great Administration Departments
in the region or any states in the Middle East. The recurrence of the Tunisian experience in the Middle East took everybody by surprise. The events
of January 2011 in Tunisia shook the world, as nobody expected such developments. The same happened with Egypt in January 2011.The process
is not settled yet or still going on in Egypt, Yemen, and Bahrain. In Jordan,
the demonstrations had started before Tunisia and continued time after.
The demonstrators in Jordan asked for the change of the Prime Minister.
The magnitude of the reaction in the countries which witnessed ongoing
demonstrations and demands came as a surprise too.

The Number of Injured Persons Exceeded 2,000

Here are the main aspects of the developments in the Middle East in general (these are notes):

1. The governments did not expect these developments. They were
    completely unaware of what was going on. As a matter of fact, they
    were in complete darkness

2. Since the number of casualties was very high, the demands of the pressure groups amplified. For example, at the onset of the events in Egypt, the number of victims was over a hundred persons. The number of injured persons exceeded two thousand. However, the number of victims may have actually been higher because people are afraid to report victims to the authorities. In Tunisia, the number of those killed exceeded 200 people. In Libya, in the first four days, the number of victims surpassed 200.

3. The participants were from the capital city and other cities in Tunisia, Egypt, and Jordan. In Egypt, the demonstrations took place in Ismalieh, Suez, Alexandria, Bani Swayef, and other cities.[3]

4. To my knowledge and the archives of the *Addustour* newspaper, the participants were ordinary people. They were part of the pressure groups but not members of political parties. History will have to record a new phenomenon in the Arab World, namely the role played by pressure groups rather than political parties or intellectuals holding various prominent positions.

Historic Development

Moreover, the role played by pressure groups in the Arab World has precedence. For instance, in Jordan, pressure groups have had a significant role overtime. Yet pressure groups in Egypt, Bahrain, Libya, Yemen, and Tunisia have had no impact, historically.

The Arab countries that witnessed the so-called Arab Spring demonstrations are traditional allies of Western states and their leaders; the Presidents of Egypt, of Tunisia, Yemen, and the King of Bahrain have been their friends in the region. Only Syria is an exception. Most of these leaders have been accused of corruption and inefficiency in running the business of their countries.

The Governments Resorted to Gangs

The protests showed that the systems in Egypt, Libya and Tunisia were aloof from their people and unaware of their hatred. The governments resorted to using gangs to kill their protesting civilians. Because of this, the number of victims was high and the people's demands increased. In Egypt and Tunisia, the police attacked the protestors. The government was accused of using sharpshooters to kill its people. Gangsters and the secret police were accused of involvement, of disguising themselves in civilian clothes and attacking the protestors. This first happened in Tunisia, then in Egypt and later in Libya. The Libyan government, according to statements made by Libyan citizens, opted for the services of foreign mercenaries.

People and Gangs

This was not the case with Jordan. On 18 February 2011, the people of Amman complained of having been assaulted by gangs, who attacked them after the Friday prayers at El Husseini Mosque downtown, whilepolice did not intervene. The government reacted promptly to remedy the situation. The government created a committee entrusted with the task of investigating the circumstances of the case. During future demonstrations, the police forces of Jordan handed out soft drinks and bottled water to demonstrators.

Secret Police

In one of the Egyptian cities, people got hold of 63 persons who were vandalizing and stealing. They handed them over to the Army. Three of them were carrying ID Cards showing they belonged to the Secret Police. There was fabrication of information by the government. The Centre of the National Party (The party of the President) in Cairo was not set on fire by the people, because it actually burnt from the inside and the upper floors. In Tunisia, people spotted foreign cars with temporary plates attacking people. In Egypt, people claimed that they saw cars with diplomatic plates doing the same thing. In Tunisia, people claimed Israeli sharpshooters placed on top of buildings shot at the leaders of the demonstrations and killed them. I doubt that they were Israelis but rather European mercenaries. All demonstrators were acting peacefully. The agitation and brutal killings came from the governments in both Egypt and Libya. The same happened in Yemen, Bahrain, and Tunisia.

The Removal of the Ruler

The reaction of the governments of Egypt, Tunisia, Bahrain, Yemen, and Libya was by far too tough and in return, the reaction of the people was not soft. The governments of Egypt and Tunisia lost control and the leaders of these two states fled their countries in less than a month. I think the situation in the countries where violence occurred is difficult because the governments used violence to try to control the people. They ordered the secret police to attack civilians. Hundreds were killed. As a result, the pressure groups' demands amplified and demanded the removal of the ruler. The same happened in Egypt. Egypt is very similar to Tunisia; the middle class is still frustrated. By the end of the year, the demonstrators were comprised of the poorest class. They were not part of the class that took part in the events of January 2011. There is still a lot of corruption. Today, businessmen rule the country under the umbrella of tyrant leaders in the same manner they run their businesses.[4]

The leaders now enjoy great confidence and they have lost motivation for reform. They are confident they are protected by Western powers like the USA, which no longer calls for reforms in Egypt, Tunisia, or elsewhere in the Arab world. People are fed up with these double standards. For example, on Wednesday the 16 February 2011, President Obama talked about human rights in Iran and ignoring totally other states.[5]

The Methods Practiced by Pressure Groups and the Methods Practiced by Governments: Sharpshooters

The middle class started the protests peacefully and continued this way even when they raised further demands after the government used gangs to crack down on the demonstrations. Sharpshooters were commissioned to kill civilians. This immoral action was carried out by the Egyptian, Bahraini, Libyan, and Tunisian governments. In Egypt alone there were over 365 victims in the first few weeks. The number of victims in Tunisia is a bit less. Until 21 February 2011, the number of the victims in Yemen was high and several wounded. In Libya, the number of victims went beyond hundreds, according to people interviewed on Al Arabia TV. Some claim there were 35,000 mercenaries, mainly from Chad, in Libya. There were rockets fired in the Eastern part of the country. A Commando Brigade joined the demonstrators. Half of the country collapsed. On 21 February 2011, Gadhafi's son appeared on TV in a very unconvincing way—he was threatening the people, but the people were no longer afraid. An Arab proverb says that a drowning person is not afraid of getting wet. In Bahrain, the demonstrators were exposed to the guns of the police. One person was killed. During that victim's funeral, another person was killed. Consequently, the king addressed the people to placate their anger. Nevertheless, after his speech another three people were killed by the police. As a result, the demonstrators' demands escalated and they requested the institution of a constitutional monarchy. They demanded an elected Prime Minister and the cessation of discrimination.[6]

The circumstances in Bahrain are different from Egypt and Tunisia. In Bahrain, the matter is not corruption or poverty. It is freedom. The Shiites think the government is giving nationality to Sunni foreigners to balance or increase the Sunni presence in Bahrain. They claim the population's census increased in 2008. The events continued to spiral in 2011.There were more victims. In Libya, the situation deteriorated after demonstrators demanded the removal of the president in front of his supporters. Events were escalating every minute in the Arab World. Most of the countries witnessing demonstrations of pressure groups were friends of the USA. The people in Egypt, Libya, Yemen, and Tunisia hated their rulers, and accused them of being the puppets of the Western regimes who humiliated them for the last 20 years after the collapse of USSR and the occupation of Iraq.[7]

The Developments Reveal the Weakness of the Administration

The new role has been assumed by the pressure groups in the Arab World due to the weakness of the Official Departments. This is a recurrent experience in the Middle East. In April 1989 Jordan did not expect the uprising either. The uprising in Tunisia in January 2011 was very strong. No one expected it. The same was the case with Egypt in 1977 too. The demands of the demonstrators in Jordan asked to change the Prime Minister. The amplified reaction in Jordan was unexpected too.

Notes About the Lessons which May Be Learned

- The governments did not foresee the events. Protests had happened before when the revolution took place in Iraq in 1958. Iraq was the Centre of the Baghdad Pact. Nevertheless, the British and the Iraqi governments had no idea what was going to happen. They were in complete darkness although they had the strongest intelligence departments in London, Washington, Ankara, Tehran, and other capitals.

- The number of the victims was high in Cairo and other cities in Egypt during the first days of demonstrations (there have been no victims in Jordan however). There were more than a couple of hundred victims in Cairo alone. The number of injured persons exceeded two thousand. The number of victims could be more because people were afraid to report the number of casualties to authorities. In Tunisia, the number of the victims exceeded 200.

- In Tunisia, Egypt, and Jordan, the demonstrators were from the capital as well as other cities from around the country. In Egypt, the demonstrations occurred in Ismailia, Suez, Alexandria, Bani Swayef, and other cities. In Libya, the demonstrations started in the Eastern part and extended to the capital.

No Impact to the Parties

- The participants were ordinary people. They represented pressure groups not parties. The parties or intellectuals holding prominent positions had no impact. In the fifties, the changes in the Arab world were carried out by officers backed by Western powers. This was the case of Egypt in 1952 and Syria after the 1948 war with Israel. Later on, the officers who instigated the revolutions in Iraq on 14 July 1958, Yemen in 1961, and Iraq in 1963 were backed by Egypt.

- The role of pressure groups in Jordan has been obvious in its history, whereas the role of the pressure groups in Egypt and Tunisia was a novelty.

- The states that witnessed the demonstrations as well as their leaders, like the Presidents of Egypt and Tunisia, are allies of the Western states. In Jordan the demonstrators criticized the prime ministers, not the king. In the early days of 2011, the Prime Minister of Jordan was accused of corruption and inefficiency in running the country's affairs.

- These developments proved that the systems in Egypt and Tunisia are immoral. In Egypt and Tunisia, the police attacked the people in various ways. Sharpshooters killed people. Police wore civilian clothes and attacked the people too. This happened in Tunisia, Libya, and Egypt. In one of the Egyptian cities, the people caught 63 persons who were vandalizing and stealing. They handed them over to the army troops who were scattered over the cities. Three of them were carrying ID Cards showing that they belonged to the Secret Police.[8] The Centre of the National Party (the party of the President) in Cairo was not set on fire by the people because it was burned from inside and the upper floors. In Tunisia, people saw foreign cars with temporary plates attacking people. In Egypt they spotted cars with diplomatic plates doing the same thing. In Tunisia, they claimed Israeli sharpshooters placed on the top of the buildings shot and killed the leaders of the demonstrations. I doubt that they were Israelis, but I should think they were European mercenaries.

- All the demonstrations were peaceful. No riots or agitation occurred. The agitating and brutal killings came from the government sides in Egypt and Tunisia.

POST TUNISIAN ERA

Leaders in Tunisia, Egypt, Bahrain, Yemen, and Libya Conceded to Slight Concessions, But Not Reforms

In Egypt, pressure groups went out to react against humiliation and the poor living conditions, created by the class of fabulously wealthy businessmen. For instance,[9] Mubarak's wealth, the Egyptian President, was estimated at $75 Billion, whereas President Qaddafi's wealth was estimated at $1,500 Billion. The further development of events in Egypt is the outcome of their leaders' conduct.

- On 19 January 2011, the Egyptian President changed the government and promised to go ahead with reforms. Nevertheless, people kept on expressing their hatred towards the regime and the ruling party. They burnt down the centers of The National Party, President Mubarak's party. Subsequently, the government declared curfew. In the absence of security forces, the army scattered in cities.

The Egyptian army is as large as 468,000 soldiers. It is the tenth largest army in the world. The number of security forces amounts to 1,400,000. The people protesting in Egypt represented two-thirds of the population of Egypt. Today, some 90% of them are not working according to the press.

- On 30 January 2011, Mubarak appointed a new Vice President, Omar Suleiman. The Egyptians accused Omar Suleiman of being a CIA agent, and of having facilitated the American invasion of Iraq. He was also accused of having assisted the Americans in interrogating the prisoners kidnapped by the CIA and the American Forces from Italy and Afghanistan with the purpose of establishing a relationship between Sadam Hussein of Iraq and El Qaeda. They made references to the book *Patton's Madness* by Jean Mayer and referred to Omar Suleiman, the Head of Intelligence Department at that time. Consequently, Mubarak appointed Ahmed Shafeeq (70 years of age) as Prime Minister. He had been a pilot and the Minister of Aviation for years. In December 2010, *The Wall Street Journal* mentioned Ahmed Shafeeq as the one to replace Mubarak. Both Omar Suleiman and Ahmed Shafeeq were abhorred by the people. Omar Suleiman disappeared after the departure of President Mubarak.

- On 31 January 2011, on the sixth day of the crisis in Egypt, the number of the victims rose to 160. Some leaders in the Arab World like the King of Saudi Arabia and the Prince of Kuwait expressed their support of Mubarak. Police returned to the streets of Egypt. Mubarak ordered the resignation of the Minister of Interior.

- 1 February 2011, Mubarak declared he would not stand as a candidate for the Presidency in September. As a result, there was a call for one million demonstrators in Egypt. Meanwhile in Syria, President Assad declared Syria was over this political instability and opened the gates for foreign banks and private universities.

- On 2 February and 3 February 2011, the ninth day of the uprising in Egypt, secret police attacked the demonstrators riding on horses and camels. The demonstrators had declared that Friday would be the day of Mubarak's departure. The famous Egyptian religious Sheik of Qatar's Al Jazeera, Yousef Gharthawi, supported the departure of Mubarak.

In the meantime, in Yemen the President declared that he would not nominate himself for presidency again. However, this declaration did not appease the people as it came too late. On 20 February 2011, he declared he would allocate 60,000 jobs to the youth. But the people did not believe or trust their leaders anymore.

- On 3 February and 4 February 2011, the heart of Egypt was burning. Demonstrators in Alexandria demanded the hanging (death sentence) of Mubarak. Some 149 UN officials left Egypt for Cyprus to avoid the instability. The demonstrators caught 120 persons from the secret police and members of the National Party who had dressed in civilian clothes attacked the demonstrators. The situation was getting chaotic. Foreigners were not welcomed anymore. People did not trust foreigners any longer and a foreigner was killed. The people handed the suspected foreigners over to the police.

- Friday 5 February 2011: The Friday of Departure. Two million gathered in Cairo, Alexandria, and other cities of Egypt. Just a few supporters of Mubarak gathered. Different entities exerted pressure on Mubarak to leave or delegate his power. A new committee emerged. This committee, comprised of wise people from several sides, demanded Mubarak delegate his power to his deputy. Mubarak refused to leave, claiming he did not want to plunge the country in chaos.

- On 6 February 2011, the press declared the gas line in Al Areesh, east of Egypt, had been destroyed. This line supplied gas to Israel, Jordan, and Syria. In Aqaba, Jordan, two units out of five work on gas. This station in Aqaba provides Jordan with 30% of the needed gas in winter and 25% in summer. According to Jordan Resources Department, Jordan imports 230,000 cubic meters daily. According to foreign sources, Israel gets 60 billion every year, whereas Jordan gets 8.5. On the same day—called the Day of Martyrs in Egypt—despite the heavy rain, a large number of people, although less than before, streamed to Tahreer Square, Abdil El Muniem Riadh, and some other streets hosting the governmental departments.

In Egypt, people are angry because Israel buys a unit of $2. A few years back the people went to court and got a court decision not to export gas to Israel at this price, but later on they lost the battle at the Administrative Court level.

This is a summary of the developments in the post Tunisian era, which lead to the change of the regime in Tunisia and Egypt, and it was the beginning of and followed by the change in Libya and Yemen.

The regime in Egypt and the neighboring states have conceded the following. In Jordan, the King was quicker than the government in containing the escalation of events and prevented the situation from getting worse. He distributed food packages to needy families and prepared three roving hospitals to remote areas where Bedouins live such as the Maan district, in the North and Middle Desert areas. The King increased the salaries of the army and public employees and raised pensions by 20 JD (30$). The King visited two poor villages in remote areas of Jordan and furnished the houses of these two villages with furniture. The Queen actively promotes educational workshops. Moreover, the king appointed a new Prime Minister and urged him to take special care of the youth. The Prime Minister pledged to combat corruption. The King visited more remote villages in the Eastern desert and assisted the poor people in those areas with housing and medical treatment. The Queen frequently meets women from underprivileged quarters in Amman.

The Problem is Poverty and the Corruption of the Ruling Business Class

In Jordan, people rose up to protest high prices. On Sunday 16 January 2011, the government declared a price cut of yoghurt, sugar, and imported meat. But the people were reluctant to acknowledge this measure and claimed the prices were the same. On 22 January 2011, the King declared he would raise salaries with 20 JD ($28).[10] Before the collapse of the Tunisian government, the Jordanian government reduced the price of fuel, which had been increased two weeks earlier. Nevertheless, the people started to demonstrate against the government and demanded the departure of the Prime Minister.

There were demonstrations in Amman and outside the capital in Jordan. The demonstrators asked for changes in the legislative system like reforms and the changing of the election law. The real problem in Jordan, Egypt, Tunisia, and Yemen is the problem of the middle class, which is affected by impoverishment and unemployment. At the same time there is a ruling business class which has no stomach for reforms. So, poverty. along with corruption, which reached its peak in Egypt, Tunisia, and Libya at the presidential level while in Jordan at the ministerial level, are among the factors that led to the uprisings. In the case of Bahrain, discrimination the lack of freedom and motivated pressure groups to stand up.

The Palestinian Issue

All these accidents occurred after Israel and the USA failed to find a resolution in the peace process negotiations. Egypt discovered that an Israeli spy network had infiltrated the communication infrastructure in Egypt. The scandal, provoked by WikiLeaks in the Arab world and the role played by the USA, shattered the image of a benevolent America.

The Awakening of the People and the Slight Concessions Made by Leaders

In some Arab states like Egypt, Tunisia, and some other countries, there are presidents and prime ministers who think they are immune to public pressure and should rule forever. They ignore the need for reforms and do not respond to the demands of the people. Day after day the frustrations of the people and the hatred towards their rulers soar. There is tension in Egypt because the leadership has not conceded to the continuous demands. This is also the case in Yemen. Libya is experiencing a similar problem. The only exemption is Tunisia where the demands are taken in consideration. By the end of 2014, they had peaceful elections. The pressure groups are still there waiting for the reforms.

Notes

1. Addustour is a Daily Political Independent Newspaper and is one of the important papers in Jordan (Amman- Jordan).

2. The researcher used the archives of Addostour.

3. Ibid; and BBC AT 9 AM 30th JAN 2011.

4. Addustour archives; and on 29 January 2011, a journalist talked to BBC.

5. Addustour 17 FEB, 2011.

6. Addustour 22 FEB, 2011.

7. Addustour archives.

8. On 29 January 2011, a journalist talked to BBC.

9. On 20 February 2011, according to speakers of Arabia TV.

10. Addustour Newspaper.

CHAPTER 4

The Bargains Diplomacy in the Syrian Crisis

Why is the Syrian Crisis Different?

Russia has been the main player in the Syrian crisis since it started in 2011. Her main goal is to protect her interests by supporting the regime in Syria. She mobilized her efforts politically in UN and mobilized the efforts of China to assist her in the coming battle. On the regional level, Iran has the same goal as Russia. For Iran, the future of Hezbollah in Lebanon depends on the fate of Syria. For Iran and Russia, the conflict in Syria is zero sum game. That is the main reason in my opinion that makes the Syrian crisis different from the other crises in the area. The other side in the Syrian conflict doesn't have the same motivation. The conflict for the opponents of the Syrian regime, on the other hand, is not zero-sum game. Russia and Iran have participated in the Syrian conflict directly. The US depended on regional allies in military operations. Turkey and the GCC claims the US distributed their efforts. Some participated by supporting the Syrian opponents by money like some of the GCC. Others sent weapons. Turkey paved the way for the insurgents. Turkey's door was open for the insurgents from all over the word. The borders were open for those who wanted to leave Syria. Some insurgents got involved in stealing the oil, antiques, and the Syrian factories. Syria has avoided the fate of Libya because she has very strong bilateral relations with international powers like Russia and a regional power like Iran; she was able to survive and avoid the fate of Libya or Iraq.

The shakeup that started in some of the Arab states like Egypt, Tunisia, Libya, and Yemen in 2011 extended to Syria, but failed in changing the regime. Although the people in Syria used arms and were supported by outside money, technology, and arms, no positive change took place in Syria.

The superpowers' role is different from their role in Libya or elsewhere. The two superpowers, the US and Russia, had different goals in Syria from their goals in other Arab States. There is a real confrontation between the two powers. Iran appeared and took place in the regional conflict since 1979. Few people observed the change in the area after 1979. The development happened like this: Israel occupied Lebanon twice in 1978 and 1982. The Arab World was weak. Egypt had already left the conflict and Iraq was busy in a war with Iran.

Iran interfered in the conflict in Lebanon in an unexpected way. She mobilized the Shiite in Lebanon and founded new resistance in South Lebanon. Hezbollah was founded and became part of the conflict and resistance. A new problem appeared for the US and Israel—Syria, the old ally of Egypt, found new ally in Iran in 1973. Syria supported Iran in Lebanon; since then, Iran has built strong bilateral relations with Syria. This is one of the main reasons that enabled Iran to get involved in protecting Syria and this became one of the main goals in Iran foreign policy. This makes the situation in Syria different from Libya and Egypt or Yemen. Everything is different. When the struggle started in Syria in 2011, I expected that the allies of Syria had been more committed than the supporters of the Syrian protesters who revolted and became insurgents. The battle for changing the regime in Syria was full of expectations by the enemies of Syria that they would topple the regime in a few weeks. Half of the insurgents in Syria are mainly from El Nussra organization (front). Nussra (Organization), a terrorist organization, changed her name to Fateh El Sham (which means the Conquest of El Sham; EL Sham is the old name of Great Syria). At the same time, the leader of this organization appeared unmasked. He is Abu Mohammad El Golani, who stated that he defected from the Al-Qaeda Organization. More than fifty of the cadre of this organization are Syrians.

The Quantity of the Supporters

There is important factor which we must take into consideration. It is the quantity of the states that are fighting and supporting Syria. They are different from those who are supporting the insurgents. Another thing, beside the quality of the Syrian block, is the cause—Iran, Russia, and Hezbollah defend Syria. For them it is zero sum game. On the other side there is no cause, or the cause is not convincing. The people in Syria were scared from developments in the region. The Arabs in general don't believe that the struggle's goal is to change the Syrian President Bashar El Assad for the sake of democracy. No one believes that replacing Assad is a higher priority than the situation in the West Bank and Gaza. The priority of the lay man in the Arab World is to deter Israel there. Every Arab citizen is afraid that the change in Syria will lead Syria to the same fate of Iraq and Libya. I believe that the legitimacy of the Syrian president will be strengthened, and he may be distinguished in the Arab world if he survives to the end. Needless to say, he did not build this fame. It is his allies' efforts and the zero-sum game nature of the conflict, and they must succeed. Anyway, the basic players are superpowers that have paved the way for bargains now and later—so the fate of Syria has been decided by the bargains made after the US and her allies couldn't accomplish their goals.

The Quality of the Opponent Block in Syria and Iraq

There are several factors helped the Syrian regime to survive for six years. On the ground, the quality of the fighters in Syria is different from the quality of the Syrian insurgents who are fighting the regime. The role of Russia in assisting Syrian is visible to the public. She sent in forces and established new bases. Hezbollah, the ally of Iran, is also fighting in Syria. Iran is supporting the Syrian regime publicly. But the US is fighting by proxy—she doesn't have the same level of allies (like Iran and Russia in Syria, Iraq, or Lebanon). She had regional allies like Turkey and some of GCC states. Turkey became the supplier of the fighters to cross the borders and fight in Syria. She made it easier for them to enter Turkey without visas. Money comes from some of GCC states. But instead of backing her allies, the US accused her allies of terror. The US vice-president Joe Biden, when he visited Turkey in October 2014, accused his allies Turkey, Saudi Arabia, Qatar, and the UAE of supporting terror.[1] In public, the US and her allies made a commitment to fight Daesh (IS) in Syria. This alignment was accompanied by noise and media. Jordan, the UAE, and others joined. But since a Jordanian pilot was brutally killed by Daesh in November 2014, people haven't heard any more about Jordan participation in public.

The USA's Allies are Executives

The basic important players are Russia and the USA. Each of them has allies in the region. The the allies of the US in Syria and Iraq cannot match the level of their rivals. I will cite one example: when Daesh occupied half of Iraq in June 2014, the Grand Shiite leader Sheik Sistani declared EL JEHAD EL KEFAAEI. It is a Fatwa—a religious permission to resist and start fighting. On the other side among the fighters of Daesh, you find things were not known to the average man in the street like JEHAD EL NEKAH (permission to the fighters to possess women while fighting). This permission is to motivate the youth to join. It is not respected by ordinary, real Muslims. The allies of the USA used different methods to win. They used women to attract men to fight in Syria. The US closed her eyes to the massacres which were committed by the insurgents in Syria or Iraq. She closed her eyes about the insurgents and their supporters' behavior, some of whom seized Syrian factories in Aleppo. The insurgents destroyed and stole ancient ruins. They stole oil and sold it. The massacres scared others and destroyed the image of Islam. All these things affected the future of the insurgents in Syria and Iraq. Regardless of world public opinion, people consider them gangs and savages. They accused the regime of killing the people. They killed people in a brutal way and kidnapped nuns in Syria. They used people as shields. In Iraq, they kidnapped women and sold them. They accused the regime of using chemical weapons; they were accused by UN reports of using them too. This behavior made people dislike them. They could have attracted the people to their cause, and they could have mobilized the people to fight the regime and force the president to step down.

Syrians Don't Accept Foreign Rule

I observed that all the accumulative experience in history was used by the US in Syria. Some of the extreme fundamentalists' fighters showed up in Syria. They are mainly from Saudi Arabia. This was one of their mistakes— it is unknown to the foreigner that these extremists who come from Saudi Arabia are ill matched with the Syrians. The Syrians are advanced in their culture. Syrians don't accept non-Syrians or people who are considered inferior to the Syrian to rule. This may be one of the factors which affected the unity of insurgents in Syria. For example, the Nussrra insurgents refused to join Daesh in one organization in Iraq when the leader of Daesh offered to combine forces.

Who Is Behind the Progress in Iraq and Syria?

Away from the methods of the gangs used by the insurgents, Russia, who has the upper hand in Syria, administered the battles in Syria. They are closer to international law, and they were patient enough to contain several powers. They succeeded gradually. Russians are the decision makers in Syria. They control all the parts. Iran will not resist Russia as long as her goals are the same goals as Russia to keep the regime in Syria safe. Iran is interested in keeping the line open for Syria to reach Hezbollah in Lebanon. Thus, Syria survived and avoided the fate of Libya.

Good Results for Syria

As a matter of fact, Syria improved her position when she cultivated the excellent results of war in Syria. She got a better position. She is protected by the Russians. Israeli jetfighters will not fly the skies of Syria and destroy military targets, accusing Syria of smuggling arms to Hezbollah in Lebanon. Now Hezbollah, who has been fighting in Syria for 5 years, has stretched his forces into Syria, which improved his strategy in facing Israel, and the situation is better than the past for him. Now Russia is in Syria, and it is not easy for Israel to attack Syria like she used to do in the past. Turkey lost a lot of her presence in Syria. She is contained too. The losses of Israel are more than anyone else's. She lost a lot.

Expected Positive Ends in Syria

The situation in Syria and Iraq is improving. There are some factors which have lead to this development. First of all, the Russian intervention in Syria is the main reason for expected positive ends in Syria. Of course there are other reasons as well, like the participation of Hezbollah and the Kurds. Both are highly skilled in fighting. There are other reasons like the Syrian government and people's style of facing these problems. Some of the reasons are the absence of Turkey after Russian intervention. So, Syria was protected by Russia. That is the reason she avoided the black days waiting for her; otherwise, she would be in a worse position than Libya.

The US engaged in all the fronts of the Middle East. By far, nothing has much affected the US position. There are no rulers in the Middle East who can broker a reunification. The US is not motivated to change policy. She is worried about Israel more than she is worried about any other state in the region. She is worried about the developments in Lebanon. She cannot bear the idea that there is power in the region that affects or reduces the power of Israel. Israel was deterred by Hezbollah. That is one of the reasons that makes the US insist reducing the power of Syria to reduce the power of Hezbollah.

So, Russia deterred these two powerful states. Now neither Turkey nor Israel can provoke Syria. Even the US cannot do that. Two months ago, the US complained that there was attack by Russian jet fighters against insurgents armed by the US in the south of Syria. When John Kerry, the US Secretary of State, raised his voice, the Russian defense Minister flew to Syria to "inspect" the important Russian base in the North, sending the Americans a message. Earlier, Russia stated that the US must have the permission of the Syrian government if they want to enter Syria. But the US, France, and the UK ignored that. They cannot ignore that for long.

The Bargains Era

I observed that Russia leads the bargain diplomacy in Syria. She demonstrated her muscles in Syria through military intervention, but she brokered several important bargains. BBC mentioned the UN report about the use of chemical weapons in Syria by both sides in 2014 and 2015.[2] The report says this comes after the crisis of 2013 when the US accused Syria of using these weapons. By then Russia was the "honest broker" who interfered to finish the crisis by making Syria get rid of the weapons, and through that stopped the US campaign to attack Syria; this was one of their great bargains. But the bargains continued after Turkey reconciled with Russia in June 2016.[3]

The Future of Syria is Decided by Bargaining

The future of Syria is being decided by bargaining now. In the last three months, there have been bargains behind the curtains that have directed events in Syria. The agreement between the US and Russia on 9 September 2012 reflects that events are directed through bargains between the prime players.[4] The bargains made on the 9th of September reflect that there are two super powers directing the events in Syria; the bargains were surrounded by secrecy. The journalist got nothing when they met the two Foreign Ministers of Russia and the US. It was supposed that Russia would put pressure on Syria and Iran at the same time. Iran was not mentioned clearly. All the other parts have no principal role. There is a secret bargain that preceded the crossings of the Turks through Syrian borders, which was called the battle of Jarablus (city on the border of Turkey) in the North of Syria, to drive Daesh insurgents from the city. That was not a battle—it was a great noise with no real fighting. It was part of bargain. It permitted Daesh to depart peacefully to Idlib or El Riqih. There will be another bargain too in the near future I expect. On August 25, 2016, there was another bargain for Daria city near Damascus. There were 700 insurgents who left Daria peacefully without heavy machines and guns. There were 4,000 civilians deported to a safe place. So there were several bargains made in a short period. On 10th September 2016, the BBC talked about another bargain to move the insurgents to safe places. The name was not decided by then.[5] But it was a bargain, not war.

In the north when Turkey crossed the borders, she declared that it was the beginning of battle—the shield of the Euphrates launched against Daesh and others. As matter of fact there was no battle. According to eyewitnesses, there were no fires. Daesh left peacefully. The Turks and their supporters advanced to dismiss the Kurdish forces. The Kurds were supposed to leave to the East of Euphrates. I expect there is bargain too that the US, Turkey, and Russia played to save the life of the insurgents. This happened in Jarablus and Daria too. In one day, the battle of Jarablus was finished. As a matter of fact, it had never started. The Kurds departed to the East, and according to US advice would stay in the East of Euphrates. In the same day, the insurgents left Daria.

So bargaining methods yielded more positive results in Syria. This increased after the reconcilement between Russia and Turkey and after the failure coup in Turkey. Turkey changed her attitude and reconciled with Russia and Iran. This was a bargain too. She changed her demands. She stopped talking about the removal of Assad. She accepted Russian or Iran ideas about this subject. The Turkish leader visited Russia and Iran. So, he is in the other camp. At the end it may be noted that bargains achieved more than wars and most of the important things were done through bargains and telephone calls, not jetfighters or tanks.

Notes

1. Russia Today (RT) broadcast on 3 OCT 2014 the accusation and the protest of UEA. Biden changed some of his accusations.

2. BBC covered the occasion in detail; 25 August 2016.

3. Russia Today (RT) covered the reconciliation on 20 June 2016.

4. BBC covered this issue in a professional way.

5. BBC interviews by Syrian Official

6. City near Damascus, President Assad prayed in it in the Eid Al Adha on 12 SEPT 2016.

PART 2

CHAPTER 5

Tribes, Land and Administration in Jordan, Past and Present

1. Interaction between tribes, land, and government
2. Quraish tribes
3. Ottomans and tribes
4. Swiss Canal and tribes
5. Huwaytat tribes and World War 1
6. Glubb Pasha and tribes
7. Tribes and the safety valve
8. Globalization and tribes

A Summary

This research concentrates on the interactions between the tribes with the administration in Jordan all over the years since the dawn of Islam up to date. There were always interactions between the two entities: the tribes and the administration. This study assumes that this element has been the most important safety valve for stability. The study follows the interaction between three elements: the tribe, land and the government. The most important element among the three is the tribes. Sometimes they were a benefit and other times a constraint on decision making. The Ottomans took this factor into consideration. Other governments have done this before. This study reaches the conclusion that the tribes through all the years were the safety valve in Jordan.

Introduction

Perhaps very few people recall that the initial spread of Islam was carried out by Bedouin armies. Any new empire or state, according to Ibn Khaldoun, needs powerful groups to enforce the law. When the new state emerged in Madina—Yathrib—the Prophet Muhammad (bless his soul) depended on Islam to unite the scattered tribes. He succeeded in uniting them into one group, which became *asabieh*. *Asabieh*, according to Ibn Khaldoun, is the power which every new state needs, and it means the power of groups, tribes or big families (Ibn Khaldoun 1978). The Prophet was able to protect the new state by uniting the *asabiehs* (plural of *asabieh*).

Because Jordan was on the route between Damascus and the holy places of Mecca and Madina, Jordanian tribes enjoyed a special position as hosts receiving guests and protecting their caravans as mentioned in the Holy Qur'an. The verses say in the Quraish Surah:

لِإِيلَٰفِ قُرَيْشٍ ۝ إِۦلَٰفِهِمْ رِحْلَةَ ٱلشِّتَآءِ وَٱلصَّيْفِ ۝ فَلْيَعْبُدُواْ رَبَّ هَٰذَا ٱلْبَيْتِ ۝ ٱلَّذِىٓ أَطْعَمَهُم مِّن جُوعٍ وَءَامَنَهُم مِّنْ خَوْفٍۭ ۝

> *Since the Quraish have been united,*
> *United to fit out caravans' winter and summer,*
> *Let them worship the Lord of this House,*
> *Who provided them against destitution and gave them se-*
> *curity against fear. [106:4]*

(Ahmed Ali 1984 contemporary translation of the Holy Quran)

The Quraish who lived in Mecca were the dominant tribe in Arabia that represented the Arabs. Its economy depended on trade. The caravans of the Quraish mentioned in the Qur'an moved between north and south. In summer, the caravans used to move towards Damascus in the north, and in winter, the caravans would move towards Yemen in the south. The Prophet Muhammad is reputed to have passed through Jordan twice as a merchant on his journey. This road, which is still used today, was the great pilgrim road to Madina and Mecca.

Jordan's prosperity is related to its location on the route between Damascus and the holy places of Mecca and Madina. When the newly founded Muslim-Arab Empire moved to Damascus, the prosperity of Jordan continued. The Jordanian desert became a favorite place for the Caliphs. The pilgrim road became unused when the Abbasids succeeded the Umayyads because their capital was Baghdad, and they used a new road to Mecca and Madina.

Jordan's importance was renewed when the Ottoman-Turks gained power. The main pilgrim route from Constantinople to the holy cities of Mecca and Madina passed through Jordan. Tribal chiefs in Jordan ruled as semi-independent *sheikhs*. The tribes were always beyond control. The town dwellers were not completely protected by the Ottoman administration, since the Ottoman system of government generally protected principal cities, such as Damascus and Aleppo, and the areas between eight and thirty kilometers from the center of those cities (Sinai and Pollack 1977).

Many sources say that the settled population was mistreated by the nomadic tribes, to whom they were forced to pay *khawa*-tribute (Abujaber 1989). This is not necessarily true because we can sometimes find evidence of a form of confederation between tribes and the settled population. For example, in the south of Jordan there was a confederation between a strong tribe called the Huwaytat and city dwellers in Ma'an and other small towns, and another confederation between a strong tribe called Bani Atyieh (the sons of Atyieh) and city dwellers in El-Karak and other small cities. Small tribes or city dwellers used to pay *khawa* when they were weaker than their neighbors. They got protection in return; so there were some mutual benefits to be had from this arrangement. The nineteenth century witnessed a purely nomadic tribal involvement in agriculture. *Sheikh* Sattam Ibn Fayiz from the Bani Sakhr tribe was the first pioneer (El Fayez 2007). *Sheikh* Sattam, who was born in 1830, became *Sheikh El-Masheikh*—Paramount *Sheikh*—of Bani Sakhr in September 1881 and governor of Zizia (Jiza under the Ottomans) until his death in 1889. Because *Sheikh* Sattam had eleven brothers and eight children, financial pressure forced him to look for other income opportunities apart from *khawa* or *ghazu*—raiding—against other tribes. *Sheikh* Sattam was successful in finding a new source of income from the Ottoman administration, which appointed him as governor of Zizia. In time, he became a farmer and gradually disengaged himself from the old tradition of Bedouins that depended in their income on *khawa* or *ghazu* (Abujaber 1989).

The Ottomans used to grant *sheikhs* of Bedouins *surra*—purse—to protect the caravans which used to move from north to south and vice versa. *Surra* was money paid by the Ottomans to the Bedouin tribes to protect the pilgrimage caravans. After the Ottoman Sultan Saleem had the ceremonial honor of receiving the keys of the holy shrines in Mecca and Madina in 1517, he started to send *surra* to the Bedouin tribes through the cashier, *ameen es-surra*. At the beginning, it was sent via Cairo to the poor people in Mecca and Madina (Abidl Rahman). Later the Ottoman Sultan sent it to the *sheikhs* of Bedouins and others, who then helped to facilitate the journey of caravans that used the route from Damascus to Mecca and Madina, protecting them on their way.

The Developments of Events in the 17ᵗʰ Century

In the seventeenth century, there was an imbalance among the tribes. This was partly because there was an absence of tribal power after the Mawali tribe near Aleppo and others disappeared from the region. The Anaza tribe was encouraged to move to the north. There were attacks on the pilgrimage caravans and *jardih*—fortified caravans. The Ottoman invented, in 1757, a way to protect the caravans by establishing a new position of *Ameer*— prince—*El-hajj* or *Ameer Dimashq* to protect the pilgrim route from Hama (in Syria) up to El-Ola (now in Saudi Arabia) (Barbir 1980). This increased the activity of *jardih*.

Jardih was an armed caravan that was used to carry food and meet the pilgrimage caravans when they returned from the holy cities of Mecca and Madina. It used to meet them in Ma'an (El -Moradi). During the period from 1531 up to 1671, there were no attacks by tribes on the caravans. This was a period of one hundred and forty years (Barbir 1980). Maybe the tribes ceased to be a threat because there was government interest in their activities. The following incident may explain the reasons for the renewal of attacks by tribes.

In 1757, a *jardih* was exposed to attack by Qadan Al-Fayez. Another *jardih* was also defeated. The Bedouins robbed a pilgrimage caravan which was loaded on 20,000 camels (El-Moqtatuf 1909). The reason for the attacks was related to weak administration. Damascus suffered a period of instability because the rulers of Damascus changed 80 times during the seventeenth century. You might say the same things about Aleppo (Holt 1966).

There were changes during this century in that *surra* was usually sent via Damascus on the 12ᵗʰ of the holy month of *Rajab* every Hejri year, and it was paid to Bedouins as a reward for using their camels. If the government stopped paying *surra*, the Bedouins would create trouble. However, A*meer El-Hajj* Hussein Maki made several errors. He suspended giving *surra* that year to tribes. This factor was the direct reason for the attack on the *jardih* in 1757 (Rafeq 1970).

The Importance of the Jordanian Tribes

The importance of tribes was apparent at the very beginning of Islamic history; for example, three prominent tribes backed the Muslim soldiers in the first battle in Islamic history which was in Mutah in the south of Jordan

(Ibn Hesham). The battle was between the Islamic troops and the Romans. The Prophet Muhammad (God bless his soul) placed importance on blood relationships. He sent to the Beli tribe in the north his famous follower (*es-sahabi*) Ummr Bin El-Aass. The reason the Prophet selected him was not only his qualifications but also because his mother was from that tribe (Ed-Dabgh1979). The mission succeeded.

The Ottoman administration wanted reforms—*tanzimat*—in the early eighteenth century and started its effort to settle the tribes in Rakka in south-eastern Anatolia and in *vilayet* of Zor—Deyrizor.

After the era of reforms in 1840, new units of administration were established. In the new administration, there were military and civilian responsibilities in the sub-districts. In the administrative structure, there were *vali* (governor), *mutasarrif* (sub-governor), *kaymakam* (district-chief) and *nahiye müdürü* (administrator of *nahiye*).

The administration wanted to force nomads to settle by establishing new *vilayet*s and *sanjak*s—lower administrative divisions under *vilayet*—and by founding new military units. There were developments in the area when the Suez Canal was opened in 1867. Control of the Red Sea had been fully monopolized by the Ottomans up until then. The Ottomans expected that the British would compete with them to control the Red Sea and would create difficulties in transportation of Muslim pilgrims—*hajj*—and merchants via the Red Sea. A few years later, the Ottomans established a *vilayet* with Amman as its center to strengthen the security in the area. They sent the Circassians to settle in the Amman area (Foundation for Studies on Turkish Arab Relations 1990); the migration started in 1878.

The plan also aimed to encourage the Bedouins to settle and to create towns for the settlement of Circassian immigrants. Moreover, it aimed to change the economic system by encouraging raising cows, instead of camels, and cultivating rice and cotton in the environs of the River of Jordan.

Regardless of whether the *vilayet* was established or not, the Ottoman expectations came true as the British occupied Egypt in 1882, and the *Vilayet* of Amman received immigrants from Egypt. This *vilayet* covered a huge area and contained most of the Jordanian tribes—that is, Huwaytat, El-Adwan, Bani Sakhr, Bani Atyieh, Bani Hamida, Ed-Dajih and others.

The Difference Between the Approaches of the El-Adwan and the Bani Sakhr in Dealing with the Administration

There was a difference in dealing with the administration of El-Adwan tribe and the Bani Sakhr tribe because the former was semi-nomadic in the Ghor area, but Bani Sakhr was nomadic and moved from place to place. The transportation facilitated the control of El-Adwan and it was also easier because they were close to the center of administration in Es-Salt city and other such places, while it was difficult to chase Bani Sakhr who used camels and entered deep in the desert (As-Shuwayhat).

These two tribes protected the pilgrim roads and the travelers in their areas. Fandi Ibn Fayez of the Bani Sakhr tribe, for example, went to the British Consulate in Jerusalem and made a deal with a British traveler Henry B. Tristram, who was going to travel to the Dead Sea and El-Karak. Tristram could not move without protection of the tribes. That was for eight thousand piaster, two guns, eleven sheep, coffee, and tobaccos. A similar agreement was made between the El-Adwan tribe and a British engineer Claude R. Conder, who also came to the area and was protected by El-Adwan (Tristram 1873).

The El-Adwan tribe had protected Tristram on his previous trip when he came to the north of Hisban. El-Adwan was his protector there because tribes divided the area geographically among them. Bani Sakhr could not protect him in the areas of El-Adwan and vice versa. *Sheikh* Sattam of Bani Sakhr went to Jerusalem to accompany Tristram to Moab, which was not under the control of El-Adwan. But El-Adwan would not allow Sattam to accompany the traveler and protect him in their area, so when El-Adwan thought that Bani Sakhr cheated them by breaking the unwritten rules of dividing the areas, they got upset and planned to prevent Sattam from passing through their land. But Sattam went to the south of their area without passing through any roads where El-Adwan was the protector (Tristram 1873).

Readiness of Nomads to Get Settled

There was readiness among some nomads to settle. Some of them discovered that agriculture could be a new source of wealth. Besides that, the Bedouin *sheikhs* became aware during the 1870s that the Ottoman administration was serious in its effort to control the countryside. They noticed the increase in government power and the new armament of the Ottoman Army.

In the 1870s a new weapon was available, and the Ottoman Army was equipped with it. The British consul-general in Damascus had by then written to the British ambassador in Constantinople and told him that Rashid Pasha, Governor of the *Vilayet* of Syria, in May 1869 had sent an advance force and a battalion of infantry on dromedaries carrying Snider rifles against Bani Sakhr and El-Adwan. However, the Ottoman unit had adopted the snider mechanisms in 1868. The Snider had been adopted by the British Army one year earlier after the conversion of the Enfield rifle following a design by Jacob Snider of New York. This allowed muzzle-loading rifles to become breech-loaders. This new weapon enabled the users, the Ottoman soldiers, to employ completely self-contained metallic cartridges which each user could carry with him in any quantity he chose. Because the Bedouins had only muzzle-loaders, the Ottoman administration was able to achieve a new level of firepower and to attain new prestige for its armed forces in specific and the government in general (Abujaber 1989).

Relationship between the Administration and Bedouins

The relationship between the Ottoman administration and the Bedouins varied from time to time according to the power of the administration. The power of *sheikhs* depended on this relationship. When the central administration was strong, the paramount *sheikhs* who had belonged to that administration became local leaders. But when the administration became weaker and weaker, *sheikhs* behaved like kings (Abujaber 1989).

Ibrahim Pasha, son of Mohammad Ali, the strong ruler of Egypt, imposed his orders on the Bedouins and the power of *sheikhs* shrunk. He forced them to settle in houses. C. R. Conder saw these houses many years later in 1881 (Abu Shaar 1995). The administrations of Mohammad Ali and his son were very effective in achieving that order. He protected the people in Houran, Irbid, and Ajloun, and used horsemen. He was very tough in dealing with the agitators in Balqa, Houran, and Ajloun in 1839. When the Egyptian Army of Ibrahim Pasha left the area, the Bedouins controlled the agricultural area and asked the people in the area to pay *khawa*. The farmers in the north paid *khawa*. You may see *wasim* (tribal marks), which every tribe uses to brand their animals (sheep, horse, camel, goat, and donkey) to declare ownership. These *wasim* sometimes indicate where a scope of a tribal influence ends (Abu Shaar 1995). Although the Ottoman administration increased the military forces after the departure of the Egyptian

Army of Ibrahim Pasha, the Bedouins continued to take *khawa* from the farmers, especially the strong tribes like El-Adwan or Bani Sakhr who might prevent migration of other tribes who tried to move from Nejd to the north but were contained by the confederations of some of the Jordanian tribes (Abu Shaar 1995). There was a confederation between the Bani Sakhr and the Sardiyeh tribe in the north to contain the Anaza tribe, who explored the possibility of moving to the north. Some may remember the size and power of some tribes when we talk about the number of fighters; for example, there were three hundred and fifty knights from Sardiyeh and four hundred and fifty knights from the Sarhan tribe of Bani Khalid. This confederation continued up until the first quarter of the twentieth century. It was strengthened when *Sheikh* Sattam married Sabha Bint Imraybia' El-Moalaq from Sardiyeh and she delivered three sons: Arif, Shibli, and Juryid (Al-Swarieh, 1996).

However, the future of the Bani Sakhr tribe itself was in danger after the death of Fandi Ibn Fayiz, the father of *Sheikh* Sattam, and the subsequent conflicts among his brothers, sons, and nephews. They were divided into two sides—that of *Sheikh* Sattam and his other brothers, Fayez and Fawaz. Without the help of the Ruwala tribe, Sattam could have been defeated. However, because Sattam was the *Nahiye Mudürü -nahiye* administrator, the Ottoman administration ordered him not to retaliate against the aggression of his brothers (Al-Swarieh 1996). Since his relations with the *Amir El-hajj* were intimate, Sattam used them for the benefit of his people to use camels conveying goods to the Ottoman administration. He protected the road from Imzayreeb (south of Syria) to El-Qutranih to the east of El-Karak. The Bani Sakhr settled there and started to cultivate the land and encourage others to do the same. In spite of that, they continued to get *khawa* from many of the weak tribes or farmers who were scattered in the area of the pilgrim road.

In the 1860s, there were peaceful relations amongst the confederations of the tribes. The Balqa confederation was under the local rule of *Sheikh Mashayikh al-Balqa* Ali, the son of the Paramount *Sheikh* Dhiyab. He was born in 1835 and assumed this post during the lifetime of his father. A sister of Ali, who was called Alya, got married to *Sheikh* Sattam in the early 1870s. The peaceful relations fortunately improved among the confederations of tribes after that marriage, especially when Ali granted his brother-in-law, Sattam, a very large area to cultivate. Ali was generous enough to tell Sattam to cultivate whatever land he could (Abujaber 1989). Sattam did not miss the chance to have as much as he could of the land. He, accompanied by two others, went to Umm al-Amad and fired a shot into the air confirming that it had become his possession and he had become the owner and protector of this land which his brother-in-law had granted him. He immediately moved on to Az-Zabayir, Zizia (Jiza), Zuwayzia, Umm Rummana, Manja, Julul, Huwara, Umm Qasseer, and at the end, Dulayla, declaring his ownership. By the end of the day, he owned ten villages. In turn, he allocated the villages to his tribal clans as follows: Az-Zubayir to Sahan, Um Rummana to Muhammad Hayil and Juruh, Manga to the Kunay'an clan, Julul to the Zabn clan, Huwara to Falah Shulash of the Zabn clan, Umm Qasseer to the Nufal clan, and Dulayla to Ayd Er-Rudayni in 1881, in compensation for Madaba which the Ottoman administration had given to the three Christian tribes who migrated from El-Karak to Madaba in the late 1870s (As-Shuwayhat). They spread throughout Madaba (Al-Swarieh, 1996).

New Migration and Interest in Land

The 1860s and 1870s witnessed the migration of three tribes from El-Karak to the north, ultimately to Madaba. These three Christian tribes were El-Uzayzat, El-Karadisha, and El-Ma'aya'a. Their agricultural activities expanded, and they bought more land. They become wealthy, and in twenty-five years got the *iltizam*—tax farm—of the whole of Balqa (Abujaber 1989).

It seems that either the Ottoman administration encouraged the Christian tribes to live in areas like Madaba, or they were encouraged by others who knew the importance of the area like Madaba. Some of the resources said that there was Esa Ehjazeen, a Christian from El-Karak, who was working with Eid Er-Rudayni from Imtair (Bani Sakhr). Esa encouraged the Christian tribes to demand Madaba from the administration who offered them the choice of Madaba, Er-Rajeeb, Sara, or Jelaad. In 1879 they cultivated corn in Madaba. When Eid came to have his share, they refused to give him any. Then *Sheikh* Sattam gave him Dulayla (As-Shuwayhat). The Christian tribes refused to give Sattam himself any of crops: wheat, oatmeal, and corn. They argued that they were not obliged to pay him since they had paid the government. Sattam attacked a guesthouse of the priest who sued him under the Ottoman administration in Nablus. It was not easy for the *Mutasarrif* (sub-governor) of Nablus to chase Sattam who could easily like anyone from Bani Sakhr run away into the desert. The administration enlisted for the help of *Sheikh* Ali, his brother-in-law. Ali had a personal reason to chase

Sattam because Sattam was no longer his brother-in-law, having divorced his sister. He attacked Umm El-Amad for three days without any success.

Sheikh Sattam was caught later by the *kaymakam*, district-chief, of Es-Salt when Sattam went to get his share of the presents. He was caught and sent to Nablus, where he was jailed for three months. He asked the priest to intervene. The priest mediated and Sattam was released. He was hosted by the priest who gave him three hundred pieces of gold—*lira*—in return for Madaba. After that he never entered Madaba again (As-Shuwayhat).

We can see that land was less important in the eyes of the Bedouins; for example, Hag-hoog Bin Zabn exchanged Huwara land from Falah for his daughter's hand in marriage (As-Shuwayhat). He sacrificed land for personal interest. If he had cultivated it, he would perhaps not have left it go so easily. Anyway, the Bedouins, especially the nomads, did not believe in possession of things. Although they badly needed land to feed their sheep and camels grass and water, the majority of them never possessed land or material things like money.

A British officer, J. B. Glubb, who served among the Bedouins in Iraq and Jordan during the years between 1920 and 1956 and became the head of the Jordanian Army, stated in 1939 that the Bedouins who he mixed with did not care to possess money. "They behave like socialists." They do not believe in the possession of money, which they consider to be like dirt on hands that comes and goes. They also consider that money in their hands is yours if you need it. By the same token, the Bedouins consider that they have the right to use your money if they need it. Glubb protested the opinions or views that the Bedouins were greedy. He said they were not. He added that they were a hundred times better than the dwellers of cities, who did not behave like this. On a personal note, one of the two writers of this research has noticed that one of the famous *sheikhs* in Jordan behaved in this way when he did not repay the money he borrowed from the bank.

The most appealing side of this culture is that a Bedouin will spend his life indebted to you once you do him a favor or good deed. There is a very famous proverb among the Bedouins: Ra'ei El-Awalih Ma Yel-ta-huq (راعي الاوله ما يلتحق), which may be translated as "You will not catch up with one who first does you a favor or good deed."

Relations between Attacks and Non-Payment of *Surra*

The Ottoman administration continued to send its forces to the area to keep security. The *vali* of Syria, Madhat Pasha, was very strict in 1880. Four years earlier, Bani Sakhr attacked a caravan and there was a battle between the two sides. There was another source of threat by the *Sheikh* of Adwan, Qublan, who was leading the confederation of the Balqa tribes. The *Mutasarrif* of Nablus was worried about the influence of Qublan.

In spite of all of this, the Ottoman administration attacked the local leaders. The paramount *sheikhs* became local leaders when the administration started establishing the Hejaz Railway. The administration established a camel corps to protect the railway from the Bedouins (Al-Swarieh, 1996).

Stability to the North of Qatrani

It seems that all the activities were to the north of Qatrani where the Ottoman administration concentrated on the trouble spots (Abujaber 1989) and paid money.

The income of the tribes to the north of Qatrani increased because they had animal husbandry among the Bani Sakhr tribe and their farmer partners. When *Sheikh* Sattam died in 1891, his encampments had five thousand sheep and goats and nearly five hundred cows. He and his nearest kin had a couple of thousand of the camels owned by the tribe (Abujaber 1989).

Regarding farming, the Bani Sakhr tribe and others depended on *murabiiya*, the farmers who used to receive one quarter of the crops for their works during the agricultural year (Abujaber 1989). The idea of *murabiiya* started when some of farmers came from Palestine to assist in planting the land. The farmers used to bring their tools, family, and sometimes oxen. The Bedouin *sheikhs* used to give them shelter, food, and protection, and let them cultivate the land and sometimes take one fifth of the crops. Later it was organized so that the farmers took one eleventh of the crops. Because of this, the farmer was called *murabii*, in singular form, which relates to the word quarter (Nahhas 1979). *Sheikh* Sattam was the first nomad to own the land and cultivate it with the help of partners, *murabiiya*, who came from Hauran, Samü village in Hebron, or the Es-Salt area. The area that was cultivated during the life of Sattam was to the west of Umm El-Amad because it received the highest rainfall. The size of area was twelve thousand dunams; each dunam is approximately one thousand square meters (Abujaber 1989).

The Bani Abbad tribes were semi-nomadic and the highest in number were scattered from Naur to the north of Es-Salt. Their number was estimated from the counting of six hundred tents in 1877. Since they were farmers, they reacted against the policies of the government that deprived them of their land and saved it for the immigrants, the Circassians (Al-Swarieh, 1996).

Bani Abbad knew the area. They competed with El-Adwan to control Es-Salt. Bani Abbad controlled Es-Salt before El-Adwan who were stronger and came later. The Ottoman administration controlled the two tribes later still in 1866. The administration caught the *Sheikh* of El-Adwan, Diab, and jailed him (Dawud 1996).

A military garrison was located in Es-Salt and a local committee was established to administer the area from the Zarqa River in the north to El-Karak in the south (Dawud 1996).

The Importance of the Area

Abdel-Hameed the Ottoman Sultan concentrated his administration on Syria, mainly its southern part. He felt that it was the cornerstone in his reforms and the security of this part was a very important element in the security of the whole Empire. He appointed the new *vali* Othman Nuri to Syria in order to make "*mutasarrifiyya*" in the southern part of Syria (Akasil 1986).

By then the *vilaya*, governorate or province, of Syria was divided into seven sub-provincial administrative divisions *liwa* or *sanjak*; Beirut, Tripoli, El-Lathedikeih, Hamma, Akka, Houran, and Ma'an. The *liwa* of Ma'an was divided into *qadas*-district; El-Karak, Tafileh, Ma'an, and Balqa. The borders of this *liwa* extended from the Zarqa River near Jerash down to Aqaba in the south, and the Jordan River in the west.

New Trend in Administration

Othman Nuri visited the area on the 18th of May in 1892 (the 22nd of Shawwal in 1309) and he wrote a report suggesting the establishment of *mutasarrifiyya* in the area (Akasil 1986). The reason for this was that the Sultan Abdel-Hameed wanted to strengthen relations between the center and these parts of the Empire. On the 18th of August in 1892, Othman submitted his report to the Ministry of Interior and the *mutasarrifiyya* appeared.

With this the mission, Othman was completed. The Ottoman administration chose the best employees for this *mutasarrifiyya*, and took great care to achieve success in this part of the Empire.

The *vali* Hussein Helmi was appointed to the new *mutasarrifiyya*. He started to market the new diplomacy to attract people. He paid a monthly salary for the *sheikh*s of El-Karak (El-Moqtabass 21 and 27 Dec. 1910, and Al-Qusus 1920). He appointed six teachers in El-Karak in the same period. The number of teachers was the highest compared with other sub-provinces—*liwa* (Turkey, Salname Suriya Vilayt-I 1311–1312). The population in El-Karak by then was eight thousand (El-Moqtabass 21 DEC 1910). Hussein Helmi left El-Karak after three years and was replaced by Sadeq—Pash—who suspended the monthly salary which was paid by Hussein Helmi (Al-Qusus).

But the situation improved when Rashid the new governor of El-Karak replaced Sadeq. Rashid concentrated on strengthening relations between the tribes and the Ottoman administration, by good service and efficient administration. He recruited many locals in the police to keep order (El-Moqtabass 21, and 27 Dec 1910).

The Confederation of the Tribes of Bedouins and Others

There were two confederations of tribes in the area. When the Egyptians left the area the power of tribes increased in El-Karak and the surrounding areas. The tribes of El-Karak were a threat and danger to the Egyptian Army who was in the area. The people of El-Karak thought that some other tribes were assisting the Egyptians against them. When the Egyptians departed, the tribes started to form confederations to be self-sufficient. By the middle of nineteenth century, they were strong enough to depend on themselves. The Bani Atyieh tribe who lived to the east of El-Karak joined that confederation. Two other cities joined one of those confederations, like Shobak and Ma'an —*Es-Shamie*—or the western part of Ma'an. The second confederation was the Huwaytat tribe and the cities of Tafileh, Wadi Musa, and Ma'an -*El-Hajazieh*-, or the eastern part of Ma'an (Al-Qusus, Al-sanousi 1981; Abudayeh 1989).

The Role of Confederations

These confederations increased the power of the tribes. They were not thinking of revolting against the Empire, but they wanted to protect themselves. The central administration wanted at the same time to have efficient central power. Consequently, many new laws appeared. The government was accused of weakening the positions of tribes and families (Asali 1986).

When the administration established the Hejaz Railway from Damascus to Madina, rumors spread that the central administration was increasing its force to achieve its political and military goals. The administration was accused of ignoring the people of the area after the reforms (Ali 1904).

The administration used to pay money to tribes—*surra*. After establishing the *mutasarrifiyya* of El-Karak and the construction of the Hejaz Railway in 1908, it reduced the money gradually every year from 30,000 *lira* to 24,000 in the second year, to 19,000 in the third year. Then it cancelled paying money altogether (Al-Moqtabass 5 Feb. 1911).

When A. Musil visited Ma'an on the 10th of July in 1910, he felt that there would be a revolt among the Huwaytat tribe or in Ma'an. He was told when he was asked about Huwaytat that they had moved to the west, and they wanted to revolt because the government suspended granting them their financial allowances—*surra*. The *vali*—governor—in Damascus heard about that, but he thought that the revolt would be in Houran (Musil 1926).

The Revolt of Druze in Houran

Two months before the revolt of El-Karak there was a revolt in Houran when the Druze revolted. Sami Pasha El-Farouqi, a famous military leader crushed the revolt. He was assisted by the Ruwla tribe who surrounded the Druze from the south. The reason for that revolt was that the people resisted the government's policy of recruiting their sons for the army. The leaders of the tribes in El-Karak resisted the same policies. The government's method of recruitment was to start a census of the population and to collect weapons from the hands of the people (Al-Moqtabass 5 Feb 1911). Suspending payment of the monthly salary was not the direct reason for the revolt. Although it was one of the important reasons, the administration did a lot of things at one time without taking into consideration the reactions of the tribes. The administration thought that crushing the revolt in Houran would deter others and scare them. Sami Pasha, the leader of the army units who crushed the revolt in Houran, became a powerful personality. He did not coordinate with the central administration. Instead, he coordinated with the *mutasarrif* in El-Karak directly and consulted him to collect arms, complete the census, and register the land (El-Moqtabass 1 Feb. 1911).

The *mutasarrif* behaved irresponsibility and he missed the opportunity of cooperating with the people. He ignored the real feeling of the tribes. The gap widened day after day between the administration and the people. The administration had no real information about the situation. We can see that from the prediction by A. Musil about the revolt in July among the Huwaytat tribe or in Ma'an. The administration in Damascus did not predict that accurately. It predicted that the revolt would take place in Houran and did not know that the strong tribes in the south were not satisfied with the situation. Later they revolted. Moreover, the administration predicted that crushing the revolt in Houran would deter the rest. The information of the tribes was better than the information of the administration in Damascus. The *vali* in Damascus was not happy that the *mutasarrif* of El-Karak received the orders from Sami Pasha and not from him (El-Moqtabass 15 Feb. 1911). The *murasarrif* was subordinate to the *vali* not to Sami Pasha.

Eighteen years before the revolt, the *vali* of Syria was Othman Nuri, who had written the report mentioned before, and he wrote that the people respected the Sultan and had no intention of resisting him. The *vali* by then made a lot of efforts to motivate and incentivize the people to bring them closer to the administration. But that policy changed. In eighteen years, the situation became different. The tribes were dissatisfied. The administration did not predict the size of their power. Moreover, the administration ignored their feeling and demands. After the revolt, the *mutasarrif* of El-Karak accused the leaders of tribes of being selfish and wicked (El-Moqtabass 5 Feb 1911). The *vali* in Damascus blamed El-Majali, the Bani Hameeda, and Es-Salaytieh tribes. The administration never thought of the reactions of the *sheikhs* of the tribes (El-Moqtabass 17 Dec 1911). For example, Qadar el-Majali, the Paramount *Sheikh* of El-Karak, who lost one thousand piasters, his monthly salary from the government when he lost his position in the local council in the city, was working against the administration (El-Moqtabass 2 Feb 1911). The *vali* never thought of the powerful size of the confederation among tribes. The situation in El-Karak was different from Houran where the Ruwala tribe was beside the administration and surrounded the Druze from the south (El-Moqtabass 2 Feb. 1911). But the situation was not like that in El-Karak and the surrounding area. On the 10th of December in 1910, the tribes attacked the governmental posts in El-Karak and Qutrana. Many stations of the Hejaz Railway were attacked as follows:

Name of the Attacked Station	Distance from Damascus (km)
El-Qasr	234
El-Lubn	249
El-Giza	260
Ed-Dhaba	279
Khan Ez-Zabeeb	295
Es-Siwaqa	309
Qutrana	326
Manzla	348
Frayfra	367
Hessa	378
Jurf Ed-Daraweesh	398
Anza	423
Wadi Jordoon	440

The *sheikh*s of Balqa, El-Adwan, Ajarmih, El-Fayez, Abu El-Ghanam, and others wired telegrams to the Sultan, condemning the attacks (El-Moqtabass 17 Dec. 1910).

Anyway, there was dissatisfaction among the tribes in the south, which may have been encouraged by external support from British or French powers.

Development of Events during World War I

There were great developments during World War I. The British needed allies in the area to face the German and Turks. They thought of the Hashemites who had a very strong legitimacy because they had been the rulers of Mecca since the 16th century. The Hashemites in Mecca in their turn were not satisfied with the administration of the Ottomans in the area. There were secret liaisons between the Hashemites and the British. England promised to help the Hashemites get independence. On the 10th of June, the Hashemites revolted against the Ottoman administration and issued the first communiqué declaring a new era in the area. When the Hashemites needed assistance to move to the north, their most suitable tool was the Huwaytat tribe who were scattered in the north (Obaydat, 1999; El-Najadat 1989). Without Huwaytat, the operations would have faced a lot of difficulties. From the 9th of May in 1917 to the 1st of October in 1918, Huwaytat were great participants in the battles (El-Najadat 1989).

The Hejaz Railway and Concentration of the Administration

When the military operations started, the Ottoman administration concentrated on the Hejaz Railway and worked on keeping it in their hands. The stretch from Damascus to Derra in the south of Syria was an important part of the line because after that it was split into two lines; one went to the west and the other went to the south to Amman, which was about two hundred kilometers from Ma'an, then to Madina in Hejaz. The railway was the source of power of the Ottoman Army (Mousa 1976). The administration fortified the station in Ma'an with three to eleven thousand soldiers guarding the railway from Amman to Ma'an. There were three thousand soldiers in the Ma'an station alone (Mousa 1976).

The line was safe to the north of Ma'an, but the operations of the Huwaytat to the south of Ma'an were successful. The famous *Sheikh* Odah Abu Tayeh of Huwaytat himself attacked and captured Aqaba. Huwaytat seized all the stations to the south of Ma'an from the 23rd to the 25th of April in 1918 (Mousa 1976).

At that time, there was no role for Bani Sakhr. When the British Army reached Beersheba (south of Palestine) in October 1917, it planned to move forward to the east of Jordan. The British were interested in persuading Bani Sakhr to attack or distract the attention of the Ottoman Army from behind. Money was paid to Bani Sakhr, but they let the British down on the 30th of April in 1918 when the British started operations (Mousa, 1976).

In general, the main role of the tribes in World War I and in the Arab Revolt was played by Huwaytat and in particular Odah Abu Tayeh, who entered Damascus with Faisal, the second son of Sherif Hussein of Mecca. Odah offered a lot to the revolution.

All the tribes to the north of Ma'an had roles to play later. The role of Odah started with the occupation of Aqaba and continued in other battles. He participated in the mobilization of people in the north to attract them to the revolution (Obeydat 1999).

The Role of Tribes in the Transitional Period

On the 5th of October, Prince Faisal established a military government in Damascus. Jordan was a part of this government. The British reneged on their promise to grant the independence to the Arabs. Britain and France planned secretly to rule the area after the withdrawal of the Ottoman administration. Although Prince Faisal protested, the British assured him that these procedures were temporary (Klieman 1970),

In Jordan, the *sheikhs* played basic roles to keep order. For example, in Karak, *Sheikh* Refifan El-Majali was playing a role to maintain order on behalf of the army (El-Madi 1959).

Mysaloon and After the Tension Started

On the 24th of July in 1920, Faisal, who became the King of Syria, faced the French Army. Faisal was weak away from the Jordanian strong tribes, and the Syrian *sheikhs* let him down. The famous *Sheikh* of the Ruwla, Nuri Es-Shalaan, used to receive golden pounds from Faisal up to August in 1918. Faisal gave *Sheikh* Nuri thirty sacks; each sack contains one thousand golden pounds. But when Faisal faced the French two years later in a battle, Nuri received the French army in Damascus, letting Faisal down (Mousa 1976).

After the Mysaloon Battle in July 1920, Jordan was left without any military force to protect the people. Syria was directly under the French power and Jordan was left with no administration and no military forces.

Without the assistance and the great role of sheikhs of tribes, no security could have been achieved in Jordan in that period. The British Commissioner in Palestine tried to fill the military vacuum in Jordan or to establish a police force from the tribes, but the British government refused (Mousa 1971).

The Meeting between the Commissioner and the Tribal Leaders

The British Commissioner came to Jordan and had a meeting with the tribal leaders in Es-Salt on the 21st of August 1920. He concentrated on security issues (El Zorkli 1926). After that meeting, Britain sent five officers to assist Jordanians in running the country. On the 2nd of September in 1920, one of these officers held a meeting at Um Kais. This meeting was held because *sheikhs* of Irbid and Ajloun did not attend the first meeting the previous month. Several local governments were established mainly in the north. The Bedouin *sheikhs* never thought of such local governments. This situation continued up to the date of the arrival of Prince Abdullah, the second son of *sharif* of Mecca, in Ma'an on the 21st of November 1920.

Prince Abdullah came to liberate Syria from French control, but the British Minister of Colonies met him in Jerusalem on the 28th of March 1921 and agreed to establish a new state in Jordan. On the 11th of April in 1921, the first central government in Jordan was established.

Interest in Tribes

The first government placed focus on the tribes by appointing two special ministers who were interested in tribes. In all the cabinets that were formed between the 11th of April 1921 and the 10th of March 1922, there were only two ministers, among six or seven in total, involved in the tribal affairs (El Wathaaq El Urdunieh 1984). On the 28th of January, the 5th of September 1923, and the 3rd of May 1924, there was just one minister who dealt with tribes and he was guided by Prince Shaker Bin Zaid, a close relative to the king. But the British planned to cancel this ministry to weaken the position of Prince Abdullah—later the King (Dann 1976). In 1926, the British succeeded to in removing the Ministry of Tribal Affairs called *Neyabit el-Asha'ir*.

The British Force

In 1926, the Frontier Force appeared to control the borders and security among Bedouins in the eastern and southern deserts. Prince Abdullah (later King) did not support that force. The British officers in Jordan like Kirkbride and J. B. Glubb also did not support that force because it belonged to the British mandate administration, and most of its soldiers came from Palestine (Vatikiotis 1967).

The Annexation of Ma'an and Aqaba

On the 25th of June 1925, Ma'an and Aqaba were annexed to Jordan. They had belonged to Hejaz before. After the annexation, Jordan bore the responsibility of a long border of seven hundred miles. The Frontier Force was not able to keep up the security in the desert. F. G. Peake, the head of the Arab Legion, thought of occupying Wadi Es-Sarhan to the east. The Bedouins were exposed to the danger of *ghazu* -raids- from outside. They need meadows for feeding their goats, sheep, and camels.

New Procedures in the North

The Jordanian government came up with the idea of resolving the problems of the Bedouin tribes in the north by treaties. The government signed a treaty on the 4th of March 1930 to resolve the problems between the tribes. A court was formed, with the judges being a British officer and a French officer. They met every two months (*East Jordanian Gazette* 1930).

The situation was not the same in the south and the east. There was *ghazu*. *Ghazu* was the way tribes did business, effectively exchanging livestock and other property. The British officer, Major Jarvis pointed out that fifty percent of *ghazu* had been business (Jarvis 1936). The Bedouins were accustomed to attack each other by raids to capture animals like goats, sheep, horses, and camels. The borders between Jordan and Saudi Arabia witnessed a great number of *ghazu* among the tribes. Since they crossed the borders, these raids were classed as international *ghazu*, and although the two governments wanted to reduce the number of these operations, it was not easy because the Bedouins were very good at running raids secretly. The researcher of this study met a very famous *sheikh* who told him that they used to bribe the police officers. Because of this, it took Glubb, the leader of the camel corps, two years to gain control of the borders. *Ghazu* became a thing of the past. The Iraqi tribes suffered more than any other tribes in the area because they were very rich, and were constantly targeted by the poor tribes. Ghazu has its own traditions. Not every tribe was exposed to *ghazu*. When Winston Churchill, the British Minister of Colonies in the early 1920s, blamed one of the Bedouin *sheikh*s for committing the crime of *ghazu*, he told Churchill that England was doing the same thing with the weaker states of the world and finding a lot of excuses for its actions.

The Bedouin population of Jordan was 170,000, and 120,000 of them were half Bedouins or semi-nomads, while 50,000 were pure nomads. The total population of Jordan was then between 300,000 and 320,000 (Glubb 1938, Epstein 1938). The priority of the government was to secure a climate of confidence with the Bedouins (Kirkbride 1956). Under these circumstances, J. B. Glubb entered Jordan and started the huge task of assisting the Bedouins to settle, as previously mentioned. Glubb began this great mission in the Jordanian Desert (Glubb 1948).

Some of the pioneers of the camel corps were interviewed by one of the authors and they referred to their endeavors to build and achieve security in desert (Sayer 1986). Many years later Glubb wrote: "Most of the credit for this proud record must go to the members of that First Little Desert Patrol of ninety men who by their wisdom, their devotion, to the cause in which they were engaged … [sic.]" (Glubb 1948:112).

Before the mid-1930s, there was a government class that consisted of teachers and employees. There was no Bedouin and no army officer, but gradually the desert became part of the life in Jordan. A new class appeared.

There was a very strange policy by Peake Pasha, the leader of the army, who insisted on keeping power in the hand of city dwellers but not Bedouins (Jarvis 1936, Kirkbride 1956). He had been keen to keep the power in the hand of the frontier force. However, Glubb concentrated on Bedouins. It appeared that he had been intending to keep the power in the hands of Bedouins. In 1939, Glubb replaced Peake Pasha in the army. He became the leader of the Arab Legion (the Jordanian National Army). Glubb was accused of concentrating on Bedouins. In 1956, after the departure of Glubb, the new officers got rid of the Bedouin officers who were loyal to Glubb. Because of the great influence of Egypt and its propaganda by radio in the Arab world, the king maintained good relations with the tribes and the prominent figures of their families. There were always senators from among them in the Upper House in Jordan.

In 1970, without the efficiency of the army and the loyalty of the tribes, Jordan could have faced difficulty after the Palestinian commandos created trouble for the Jordanian government, as it could not achieve security without power. In 1971, after a year of accidents in Jordan, the army achieved security throughout the whole county. King Hussein appointed his brother Prince Mohammad to be the head of the tribal council. The king felt that he needed this support. Two years later, Zaid Er-Rifai became prime minister. Three Bedouin ministers were assigned to his cabinet—a first in the history of Jordan. But there was continuous pressure from several sides to relentlessly try to minimize the strength of the tribes. Many politicians readily criticized the tribes to such an extent that it became a habit.

1970 and After

The year 1970 was a decisive year in the history of relations between tribes and the administration. The departure of the Egyptian President Gamal Abid En-Nassir was a basic factor in the weakening of the Palestinian position in Jordan and elsewhere. During the time of Gamal, the Palestinians were fanatical about him and their loyalty to Jordan was very weak. The Jordanian administration concentrated on the native population of Jordan to gain support. Gamal's influence was dangerous to the extent that the administration made continuous efforts to contain the Egyptian influence.

These were golden days for the relationship between the administration and Jordanians.

In 1970, civil war erupted. The Jordanian Army crushed the Palestinian guerrillas and kicked them out of Jordan. When they violated the rules and formed a state within a state, the king formed a military government in September 1970 and got rid of the Palestinian guerrillas.

The Tribal Council

After 1970, King Hussein Bin Talal concentrated on the safety valve of Jordanian security, the tribes. He formed a Tribal Council—*Majlis El-Asha'er*—and appointed his second brother Prince Muhammad as head of this council. This council was constituted from its members, and it operated for two years. The role of this council was:

1. To promote the standard of the tribes;
2. To submit the needs of tribes to the administration;
3. To delegate the lands of the government to the needy people of tribes, according to the laws and regulations;
4. To suggest the most suitable methods of administration to be implemented among Bedouins (*The Official Gazette* 1976).

This council was disbanded in 1976. In that year, the Jordanian administration cancelled the National Union—*El-Etihad El-Watani*—that acted as a party to unite Jordanians and Palestinians. That year also witnessed the cancellation of other laws related to tribes, such as the Law of the Tribal Courts and the Law of Tribal Supervision of 1936, and the founding of a new tribal court.

1976 and After

The year 1976 witnessed some developments that annulled the activities of 1971; for example, the dissolution of the Tribal Council and the National Union, which had tried to bridge the gap and build confidence among original Jordanians and Jordanians of the Palestinian origin. Some of the prime ministers who gained power after 1976 were not interested in tribes in the same way as their predecessors, who maintained contact with tribes, were, like Zaid Er-Rifai in 1973.

Some Tribal Reactions

There was a tribal reaction which took place in the early 1980s. Land was a common factor in the incidents of 1983. The Bani Hassan tribes in Zarqa reacted strongly against the administration which failed to resolve fairly land ownership issues in Zarqa. A similar problem occurred in the south in Ma'an in August 1983. It opened the way for demands for political participation.

From 1983 onwards, the Bani Hassan tribe participated in the government. This was part of the resolution to close the file of the Bani Hassan affairs. In Ma'an, however, the problem of land was not the only problem. There was another problem—that of trucks which were affected by the new government policies. It was then that the problems started. In 1989 the situation worsened and for the first time in Jordanian history, the people reacted against the government's decisions to raise the prices of some of the basic goods. The initiative came from King Hussein himself when he opened the door for parliamentary elections and permitted the political parties to work. Political parties had been banned since the law issued in 1957.

Another Trend of Abhorrence to Tribes

As mentioned before some of the politicians were against tribalism. For example, the head of the National Council put tribalism in the same category as racism (El-*Wathaiq El-Urdunieh* 1980).

Former Deputy of the Parliament Layth Ishbaylat, a prominent representative and leader of the opposition against the administration, defended tribalism, saying it did not weaken the administration. "Ousting tribalism does not mean adopting Western laws," according to Layth (Darwish 1990).

There was clear evidence to describe the situation in that period as abhorrence against tribes. An old Jordanian senator mentioned that two of the strong personalities in the West Bank asked the administration not to appoint any senators from the *sheikh*s of Bedouins. Their request was granted. Going back to the documents, they reveal, that on the 24th of December in 1966, the Upper House did not have any of the *sheikh*s of tribes wearing cloaks. However, the two personalities were included in that Upper House (October 1984).

King Hussein later said that he himself belonged to tribes and that it was a source of pride for him (*El-Wathiq El Urdnieyah* October 1984).

The Peace Treaty with Israel and After

The first incident after the peace treaty in 1994 between the tribal people and the administration took place on the 17th of August in 1996. The price of bread was raised. Four hundred people in El-Karak, after the Friday prayers—*Salaht El-Juma'*—demonstrated in the streets and attacked government offices and buildings (El-*Wathaiq El-Urdunieh* September 1996).

The reaction came from people with tribal background. That was the third incident following the 1983 and 1989 cases. They came from the same area for the same reasons. The king then accused external powers for intervening in matters (El-*Wathaiq El-Urdunieh*, August 1996).

In the following year 1997, the king energetically visited several cities in Jordan, in an extraordinary manner as follows:

- Mafraq on the 31st of July;
- Ma'an on the 12th of August;
- Aqaba on the 14th of August;
- Tafileh on the 18th of August;
- Ajloun on the 27th of August;
- Madaba on the 18th of September;
- Jerash on the 23rd of September;
- Zarqa on the 30th of September.

The king talked about democracy, national unity, the peace process, and sometimes referred to the old days when the people were around him during his youth (September 1997). The reader may notice that the king did not visit El-Karak. That was because he paid three visits to El-Karak on the 5th of June 1997, and that visit was preceded by his Crown Prince Hassan's visit on the 29th of December 1996. His Crown Prince stated that Jordan would be divided into three developmental areas (El-*Wathaiq El-Urdunieh*, September 1997).

The Fourth Incident

There was the fourth incident in 1998 when demonstrators went out and expressed their point of view against the government. That was in Ma'an, an area of tribal background. This time the reason was not economic, but related to Iraqi issues and supported the Iraqi government against the US policy in Iraq. The king again accused external powers on this occasion (El-*Wathaiq El-Urdunieh* February 1998).

King Abdullah the Second

On the 7th of February in 1999, King Hussein passed away. All the old files were still open. The new King Abdullah II visited some cities now and then. They were not necessarily towns of Bedouins like he did on the 11th and 18th of January in 2000. He presented the young students with some computer sets.

On the 21st of February in 2002, the king visited two small villages in the south: Qatar and Rahmeh. In Qatar, he saw a family who had been living under a tree for 40 years. The three daily meals for the family consisted of tea and bread only. The king immediately ordered the authorities concerned to build a big palm farm of about two hundred dunams (or two hundred square kilometers) for them (El-*Wathaiq El-Urdunieh*, 2002).

Are the Tribes Targets or Not?

Some people accused the government of being anti-tribes and of aiming to weaken the tribes when the security forces entered Ma'an in November 2002 to capture few persons who were accused of agitation. The government was accused of sending a message to warn the other tribes not to do the same. The prime minister addressed journalists on the 2nd of December in 2002 and said that all these accusations against the government were false (El-*Wathaiq El-Urdunieh*, 2002).

This was the first incident between the government and the people of a tribal background during the period of King Abdullah II. There were clear differences between the administrative procedures during this period and those of the previous period of King Hussein. In June 2005, the king started the old policy of visiting the Jordanian governorates, in areas such as

- Madaba on the 12th of June;
- Aqaba on the 18th of June (El-*Wathaiq El-Urdunieh*, 2005);
- The Southern Badia region on the 20th of July; and
- Ma'an on the 7th of August in 2005.

The king referred to closing the file of the events of Ma'an in 2002. The people of Shobak complained to the king that because of unemployment, they were losing eleven people every month who emigrated and left the city. The people of Wadi Musa also asked the king to resolve the chronic problem of the size limitation of many cities or villages, surrounded by land owned by the government. The government now sells them land it owns, so they can expand outside the village. The people complained that the ratio of unemployment in Ma'an Governorate was 53% and 25% for women and men respectively (El-*Wathaiq El-Urdunieh*, 2005). A further request to resolve the problem of land ownership was put to the king when he visited other governorates like Balqa on the 23rd of February in 2006 (El-*Wathaiq El-Urdunieh*, 2006).

Some Notes

The difference between the thirties and recent years is that there is no follow-up now. In 1930, Prince Abdullah (later King) wanted to teach the Bedouins. Glubb, the founder of the Camel Corps, followed up and finished the task in two years. The desert became a part of the Jordanian political life. These days, ideas are not followed up and translated into action. During Crown Prince Hassan's visits mentioned before, he proposed the idea of an old Jordanian culture whereby people volunteer to work. The word is *nakhwa* (chivalry, generosity, and sense of honor). The Prince wanted to institutionalize *nakhwa*, but no one followed up and no one volunteered to work on implementation of a plan of the ideas, so the proposal collapsed and the problems remain. This reminds us of an important technique which should be employed by the advisors who deal with the tribes. They must follow up and open the way for the two sides—the government and the tribes—to have a good communication system. The tribal element is very important as we have observed throughout the years. The Jordanian tribes were major players during the Ottoman Empire. The most dangerous revolt against the Ottomans came from the Jordanian tribes in the south in 1910. Six years later, the Jordanian tribes were the major players in the Arab Revolt by Sherif Hussein Bin Ali. Aqaba was captured by the Jordanian Sheikh Odah Abu Tayeh.

What attracts our attention is that the tribes are still the ones who react, for example, when the Jordanian government raised the prices of basic commodities in 1989 and 1996. The tribes always were and are the ones who react. These days, the tribes are suffering from very acute problems which have not been fully studied. There is evidence that the tribes demanded, during the king's visits, to find jobs for their sons. Sometimes they demanded a solution for the land ownership issue. This is a very chronic problem. All the riots that happened in Jordan in 1983 were related to this problem.

The scope of the land problem had reached a level which never seen before in Jordan. The problem is that the Jordanians never revealed this degree of concern during the king's visits. Although the king asked the people to submit some things in writing (El-*Wathaiq El-Urdunieh* February 2006), it was not done. Jordanian culture is not accustomed to such a method unfortunately.

The initiative has been lost on both sides—the government and the people. But the people are suffering and their suffering increases day after day. The land ownership problems have accumulated over the years. In the last three years, there has been a severe problem because the price of land has risen to an extraordinary level. Some of the Jordanian opinions appear in the weekly papers. Selling land has been subject to corruption at extraordinary levels in some places. On the 15th of March in 2007, a small article appeared in a Jordanian weekly addressing the administration and asking them to take action to protect their land (*Shehan* 15 March 2007). In another interview in another weekly, a concerned person declared that seven hundred thousand dunams were designated by the late King Hussein to a specific family in the north, and later they lost it to influential people who owned the land through unknown means. This kind of phenomenon in Jordanian tribal life is very dangerous. It relates to the life, dignity, and future of the Jordanians. It should be studied carefully. There are rumblings of discontent against this phenomenon, especially among the tribes who are not accustomed to writing down their problems, some of which may be significant.

Bibliography

Abujaber, R. (1989). *Pioneers over Jordan: The Frontier of Settlement in Transjordan 1850–1914.* (London: I. B. Tauris & Co LTD).

Akasil, E. D. (1986). *Establishment of the Ma'an Karak Mutasarrifiyya 1882–1894,* Dirasat Vol. XIII., No. 1.

Ahmed, A. (1984). *Al-Qur'an: A Contemporary Translation* (Karachi: Akrash Publishing).

Barbir, K. (1980). *Ottoman Rule in Damascus 1708–1758.* (Princeton: Princeton University Press).

Dann, U. (May 1976). "The Political Confrontation of Summer 1924 in Transjordan." *Middle Eastern Studies.*

Epstein, E. (April 1938). "The Bedouin of Transjordan: Their Social and Economic Problem." *Royal Central Asian Journal*, Vol. 25.

Glubb, J. B. (July 1938). "The Economic Situation of the Transjordan Tribes." *Royal Central Asian Journal*, Vol. 25.

———— (1948). *The Story of the Arab Legion.* (London: Hodder and Stoughton).

Holt, P. M. (1966). *Egypt and the Fertile Crescent 1516–1922* (Ithaca: Cornell University Press).

Jarvis, C. S. (N.D.) *Arab Command: The Biography of Lieutenant Colonel F. O. Peake.* (London: Hutchinson & Co.).

———— (1936). "The Desert Bedouin and His Future." *Royal Central Asian Journal*, Vol. 23.

Kirkbride, A. (1956). *A Crackle of Thorn.* (London: John Murray).

Klieman, A., S. (1970). Foundation of British Policy in the Arab World: The Cairo Conference of 1921. (London: John Hopkins).

Young, Hubert. (1933). *The Independent Arab* (London: John Murray), translated.

Musil, A. (1926). *The Northern Hejaz.* (New York: American Geographical Society).

Rafeq, A. (1970). *The Province of Damascus 1723–1783.* (Beirut: Khayats).

Sinai, A., and Pollack, A. (1977). *The Hashemite Kingdom of Jordan and the West Bank.* (New York: The American Academic Association for Peace in The Middle East).

The Report of the British Chief of Staff Colonel Dawney File F.O. 882/7, 1 May 1918, translated into Arabic by Mousa, S. (1976). Op.cit.

Turkey, Sâlnâme süriya vilayet-i 1311-1312 H.

Turkish Arab Relations: Annual 1990 (Istanbul: Foundation for Studies on Turkish Arab Relations).

Tristram, H. B. (1873). *The Land of Moab; Travels and Discoveries on the Side of the Dead Sea and the Jordan.* (London: John Murray), translated into Arabic by Abadi.

Vatikiotis, P. J. (1967). *Politics and Military in Jordan: A Study of the Arab Legion 1921–1957.* (London: Franc Cass).

Arabic Resources

Abdil Rahman, Ibrahim Bin. (N.D.). El-Kheyarl El-Madni, Rihlat el-Kheyari Tohfat el-Odaba wa Salwit el-Ghoraba. Cairo: Ministry of Culture.

Abu Dayeh, S. (September-December 1989). Namothag fi Dersit Tareekh wa Esool el-Ashaer. Al-Urdnieh.

Ma'an, Dirsat Tareekhieh. Damascus: Damascus University, Vols. 33, 34.

Abu Sha'ar, H. (1995). Irbid wa Gewaraha (Irbid and Its Neighborhood). Bani Obaid 1850–1928, Amman: Business Bank Publications.

Ali, M. K. (November 1904). Sikat el-Hejaz, (El-Moqtatuf).

Al-Qusus, 'A. (1920). Mudhakkirat AwdaQusus 1877–1943. (Unpublished Ms, Al-Karak).

Al-Swarieh, N. R. (1996). Amman wa Gewaraha (Amman and Its Neighborhood. Amman: Business Bank Publications). He refers to Le Strange, G. (1884). A Ride through Ajlun and Belka during the Autumn of 1884, Across the Jordan. Gottlieb Schumacher, with additions by Laurence Oliphant and Guy Le Strange. London: Richard Bentley and Son (sic).

Asali, K. J. (1988). Translator: Tahawolat Jathreih fi Filsteen: 1856–1882, Amman: Jordan University. Originally Scholch, A. (1986). Palastinain Umbruch 1856 1882, Stuttgart: Franz Steier Verlag, Wlesbaden GMBH.

As-Shuwayhat, Y.S. (N.D.). Al-Uzayzat fi Madaba, Amman: N.p.

El-Zorkli, K. (1926). Amman fi Amman (Two Years in Amman). Cairo: N.p.

Glubb, J. B. (1948). The Story of the Arab Legion, London: Hodder and Stoughton.

Ibn Hesham. (N.D.). Es-Seerth En-Nabawlch, Part One & Two. Beirut:

Dar El-Jeel.

Nahhas, S. (1979). Al-Adat Al-Arabia fi Bilad Moab. Amman: Ministry of Culture. Translated into Arabic. The original is Jaussen, P. A.; (1948). Coutumes des Arabes au Pays de Moab. Paris: N.P.

Arabic by Mousa,S. (1971). Tareekh EL-Emara) 1921–1925 and Mousa, S., 1976). Muthakarat El Ameer Zeid Amman N.p.

Obaydat, M. (1999). El-Sheikh El-Mojahid Oda Abu Tayeh, Amman: N.p.

Dawud, G. (1996). El-Salt wa Gewarha (1864–1921) (El-salt and Its Neighborhood). Amman: Business Bank Publications.

Ed-Dabagh, M, Murad. (1979). The Arab Tribes and Their Roots in Palestine, Beirut: Dar el-Taleeah.

El-Madi, M., and Mousa, S. (1959). Tareekh El-Urdunfi ElQarn El-Eshreen, Amman: N.p.

El-Moradi, M.K. (N.D.). Silk Ed-Dorar fi Ayan El-Qarn et-ThaniAshar, Baghdad: El-Mothanna Library.

El-Maqtatuf. (1909). "Sowryia fi AsrVolney." (Monthly Egyptian periodical), April 1909.

El- Moqtabse Newspaper (published in Syria). (1910). November 19, 14.

Hemedi El Fayez, Interviewed by Dr Saad Abudayeh on 30 June 2007.

El-Najadat, N.M. (1989). El-Huwayat and their role in the Great Revolt, Amman: N.p.

El-Sanousi, M. (1981). El-Rihlah el-Hejazeh, Tunisia: Tunisian Company for Distribution.

El-Wezaaraat El-Urdnieyah.Majlis El-Ummah. 1921–1984 (Jordaninan Documents: Parliament: 1921–1984). Amman: Daerat El-Matoat, October 1984.

El-Wathalq El-Urdunieh. (October 1984). Amman: Daerat El-mattboat.

El-Wathiq El-Urdunieh. (The Jordanian Documents).

CHAPTER 6

Democracy in the Middle East Concepts and Applications

Democracy is an ancient word used by the Greeks and others later to reflect the meaning of participation of the people in running the government. In Islam and in the Arab world before Islam, this word had never been mentioned. If you read all the holy Koran or read all the sayings of the Prophet Mohammad, you will never find the word democracy. If you read the poems and texts of addresses of leaders in the past, you will not find this word at all.

By the dawn of Islam in the seventeenth century, there was a very sacred city—Mecca. Although there were 365 idols in it, the Holy Temple; the House of God (Kaba) is there. Pilgrimage was one of the obligations before Islam, and after Islam it became one of the five obligations of every Moslem. The Prophet was born in Mecca in 570 and emigrated to Medina, which became sacred after the death and burial of the prophet in it in 632. The importance of Mecca is not matched by any other city. In Mecca, there was the Quraish tribe which the prophet belonged to. It had great reputation in trade because of its skill and the location of the city between the Southern kingdoms in the south Maneans and Sabena's[1] and the Northern Arabs who were in the north. There were two groups in the North. The first is in the satellite of the Byzantine and the second in the satellite of the Persians.

The City-State Polis

The Arabs before Islam had a special kind of government in the Middle of the Arabian Peninsula. It was just like the Greek Polis system. Mecca and Medina functioned according to the Polis System—the idea of the city-state. All the functions of this city-state in Mecca were divided between the subtribes of the Tribe of Quraish. This tribe played a basic role in forming all the governments of Arab states or empires later. It happens that all the rulers (the Caliphates) who succeeded the Prophet Mohammad were from Quraish. No one ruler had dared to take this title until the appearance of the Ottoman Sultans. In the sixteenth century, the Ottoman Caliphate took the title of the Custodian of the Holy Shrines. This title is still used today by the Saudi King. It has been a great honor to serve the House of God in Mecca. Even before Islam, this job was given to a branch (subsidiary) of the Quraish tribe.

Today, as a matter of fact, it participates in increasing the legitimacy of the leaders of Saudi Arabia. Leaders are looking for religious legitimacy in the Arab World, like Saudi Arabia, Jordan, and, Morocco. After 1973, the political legitimacy of President Sadat in Egypt increased, but he looked for religious legitimacy to increase his legitimacy. He failed and was killed in 1981 by religious militants.

Islam and the Social Contract

Islam practiced the theory of the social contract, which is called Baia. The Baia is an agreement between the leader and his group, which involves an oath of loyalty to him and a promise to obey him.[2]

The First Application

Abu Bakr was the first Caliphate to succeed the Prophet who left no instruction regarding his successor. He chose the title Caliphate. Abu Bakr was from Quraish and all the Caliphates who have come since then were from Quraish. An argument was raised that the Caliphate must be always from Quraish. Ibn Khaldoun resolved this problem by defining the Meaning of Quraish. He said it is *Asabieh* (power).[3]

The Qualifications of the Caliphate

Islam has concentrated on Shura as a term and as a practice. Shura is consultation with (Ahl El Hall Wa El eqid—AEHWE). This group is the inner circle of decision makers. As a matter of fact, this group has the same qualities of the Caliphate because he is one of them. The inner circle elects one of them. He must have four qualities:

- The first is the Fairness and justice because he is a judge too.
- The second is that he must be knowledgeable of the religion
- The third is that he must be Decisive and Prompt
- The fourth is that he must be enjoying good health to see and hear because he is the judge too.[4]

Quraish

There was some argument about a fifth quality. Caliphates must be from Quraish because there was a strange phenomenon that all the Caliphates came from Quraish until the sixteenth century. Ibn Khaldoun said Quraish doesn't necessarily mean blood. It means power. He used the word Asabieh.[5] As a matter of fact, he said that the history is a struggle among the *Asabieh,* so he preceded Hegel and Marx, who wrote later about dialectic and the history.

The Duration of the Social Contract

Ibn Khaldoun talked about two conditions for the duration of the Social Contract. The first he said is valid as long as the leader is enjoying good health and fairness.[6] If he is ill and cannot practice the job of efficient judge, he must be dismissed. He used the words "shortage in his body," which means if he is not able to see or hear, he will not be a good judge. The second is valid as long as he is fair. If his justice is exposed to criticism, he must resign or be dismissed by the AEHWE.

The elites or the inner circle of the leader are the same who dismiss or elect the leader (Caliphate). He is one of them. He stays in his position as long as he is fair and in good health. Regarding being fair, Ibn Khaldoun said he may be dismissed if the elites are suspicious about his fairness. He must be above suspicion.

Practically, the political system depended on Islam and specifically on Shura and the social contract, which in Islam is called in Baia. Th Baia is a social contract between the political leader and the people.[7] The people are represented by the AEHWE. The AEHWE may have small Baia and later is big Baia. Baia is the social contract between the two parts. The leader is the first part and AEHWE is the second part. This is the small Baia and there is also the big Baia. Some time the small Baia is the final Baia and the rest of people agree on it. The people always accept the small Baia.

The Procedures of the Baia

The Baia procedures are not written down. They depend on oaths of loyalty. The leader may request others (AEHWE) to take an oath to be loyal and not to let him down. The others may request the leader to be fair. They shake hands together. That is the Baia. You cannot have this with the big

Baia when there are millions of people. In Saudi Arabia among the Princes of the Royal Family, they have the procedures of Baia among the Royal family. Later on, the people may agree by expressing their consent by sending telegrams or going to the Royal Palace to congratulate the leaders, but before that there are the scholars and the men of the Shura Council, which was founded by the king many years ago, in 1926.

The Expression "The Middle East"

After World War 1 and the collapse of the Ottoman Empire, new political borders appeared and new states appeared, and a new term was used—Middle East.[8] This term was never respected by Arab Scholars, who accused other scholars who coined this expression of using this it to contain Israel, and they said the area was never East to China or Russia. It is East for the Colonial western powers.

1945 and After

When the Arab League appeared in 1945, there were seven independent Arab States. Five were kingdoms: Jordan, Saudi Arabia, Egypt, Iraq, and Yemen. Two were republics: Lebanon and Syria. In Jordan, the Kingdom adopted the Parliamentary system. There are two Councils—the upper House and the Lower House; the first is elected, the second is appointed. The King reigns, but not rules according to the constitution of 1952. Practically, however, there are not always priorities for democracy. In 1957, the King banned political parties because there were riots, demonstrations, and pressure on the government. The King always responded to developments; for example, he paved the way for freedom to speak or express a point of view by any means, written or spoken. Whenever Jordan receives immigrants from the West Bank or Palestine, the doors of freedom are open. In 1948, Jordan received the first wave of refugees. The second time he opened the doors for freedom is when he received a second wave of refugees after the 1967 war. On both occasions, he prioritized security.

In 1990, Jordan received a third wave of immigrants from Kuwait. There were 300,000 people searching for freedom. This time the experience was successful. In Jordan there are no political parties who form the government yet. But practically, there are two groups of politicians who divide power between them. Each group has men who occupy high positions in government. If the prime minister is from group A, he will choose his own men, and if the prime minister is from group B, he will likewise choose ministers from his party. Since the parties returned to work after 1992, they have never been successful. There are a high number of parties, but they are not efficient. Historically, Jordan was influenced by pressure groups that affected political life. The last successful movement by the pressure groups was in 1989, when they moved against the government (which had raised the price of food). The government responded immediately with a great wave of political reform and resuming the political parties and the elections of Parliament.

Egypt has been a Republican state since 1952. The constitution concentrated on eliminating the differences between classes, and it states that Democracy represents all classes. The constitution cancelled the parties and looked for an organization which contains all classes. In 1975, the National Union appeared, an organization to reconcile all classes of people. In 1962, the National Union appeared as a charter between all classes. Any member of the Parliament is a member in this union. It contains soldiers, peasants, and intellectuals. In 1968, members started to be elected. Its goals were declared to increase democracy. In 1971, the permanent constitution appeared. The first Council of the People appeared. Its members number 454; half of them are workers and peasants. Ten are appointed. This council legislates. The election of President is direct now. In 2005, the election of the president became a direct election. There is a consultative council founded by the president to increase democracy. It is called the Family Council and it is consultative and supervising or directing the work of journalism.[9]

Republic or Kingdom

In 1945, there were more kingdoms than republics, but since then many have been converted by military coups and have become republic states. Some of the leaders considered the changes as new legitimacy for them and they liberated the country from old, corrupt regimes. But they acted just like kings and stayed in office until they die or were replaced by another coup—nothing has changed.

The Kingdoms in the Arab World and Democracy

Now there are eight Arab states with monarchies. Six of them are in the Gulf. All of them are ruled by families; the family is ruled by Sheikh. The Sheikhs in these states are kings or princes, but they still behave like

Sheikhs. He is noble, fair, protects his people and respects them. His legitimacy is being a Sheikh. Being a Sheikh imposes many duties on him. In this case, the Sheikh never prevents his people from expressing their points of view and never humiliates them or lets others humiliate them. They came to power through the social contract, and they serve a similar role to elected leaders in Islam. In Saudi Arabia, the king always says that the holy Koran is the Saudi constitution.[10] This way, the king increases his legitimacy. In Jordan and Morocco, the kings depend on the religious legitimacy that they belong to the Prophet Mohammad. In Jordan, security was given priority many times over democracy.

In general, in the Arab world we may observe the following:[11]

1. That there is no clear role for political parties. Many states have no parties at all, like Libya or the Gulf States.

2. The role of legitimacy is not clear. Some of the Arab leaders have been ruling for 40 years. In the Gulf area, legitimacy relates to the Arab tradition of the Sheikh.

3. Protecting all kinds of freedom is clearer in the Gulf States rather than any Arab states because this relates to the characteristics of the Bedouins and the Sheikhs.

4. Regarding the republics in the Arab world, there are different titles for the government structures; for example, there are congresses in Yemen and Libya that have legislative or executive powers. Sometimes there are revolutionary councils like in Iraq and Libya. In Libya, the council controlled the government. In Algeria, the president is elected by parties. In Iraq and Syria there is only one party, the Bath party. Syria elects the president with the help of the Parliament.

There are several kinds of bodies and titles. Things are not the same and they are still changing. Democracy is a very flexible concept. After the American occupation of Iraq, this word lost its meaning in the Arab world. The Iraqis long for the old days of the ex-regime, when they had security, food, and the services of the state.

Notes

1. Dr. Hassan Ibraheem Hassan, *The History of Islam* (Three Volumes). Beruit: Ehyaa El Torath, 1964, pp. 21-44.

2. Ibn Hisham, El Sirih El Nabawieh (4 parts). Beruit: Dar El Jeel, pp. 59-79; Mohammad Hameed Allah, The Political Documents in the Period of the Prophet Mohammad and The Rashidi Caliphates. Beirut, 1985, pp. 46-48.

3. Ibn Khaldoun, *Diwan Al Mobtada Wa I Kabar fi Ayyam Al Arab wa aman Asarahum min dhabi Al Sultan Al Akbar*. Tunis, 2006, pp. 332-334.

4. Ibid., pp. 339-334.

5. Ibid., pp. 270-282.

6. Ibid., p. 391.

7. Ibid., p. 365; and Dr. Hassan, pp. 204-211; and Ibn Hisham, pp. 56-79, 225-228.

8. Y Armajani, *Middle East: Past and Present*, N J Prentice Hall, 1980, p. 1; Thomas Kavunadus, *The Middle East*, Bronxville: Cambridge Book Co., 1968, p. 1; Leonar Binder, *The Ideological Revolution in the Middle East*, NY: 1964, pp. 254-264; George Lenczowski, *The Middle East in World Affairs*, Ithaca and London: Cornell University Press, 1979, p. 8; Y. Evron, *Great Powers Intervention in The Middle East*: M. Lientenburg and Sheffter, Middle East, NY: Pergamon Press, 1979, p. 17.

9. State Information Service, Cairo: A R Publications, 2006. EGYPT.

10. The address of King Fahd on 21 June 1991, published in *Thought Perspective of King Fahd* (Ministry of Information, 2004): p. 216.

11. Fawazi Tayiem and Ata Zahra, *The Current Arab Political System*, Bangazi, 1988. Two Volumes; *The Encyclopedia of Political Science*, Kuwait: University of Kuwait, 1994, pp. 1740-1828.

CHAPTER 7

Grievances: An Aspect of Human Rights Historical Experience in Arab and Islamic Values

This study focuses on a very new idea in human rights in Arab and Islamic Culture. It is the subject of RM, Raffee El Mathalim. This means reducing or combating grievances; a decision maker practices the job of judge and executes the resolutions immediately. The assumption is that human rights in the Arab World have been taken care of in a way that has not existed elsewhere. Arabs before Islam and after Islam concentrated on the same subject.

This unique experience has not been introduced to the others in the proper way. If Islamic literature in human rights is reviewed, a very large amount of new information would be found. This paper is directed to the non Moslems and non Arab-Moslem readers who don't know about Islam and Arab culture.

After the 11th of September, writers in the Arab world were busy defending Islam in the same old way. Many conferences took place to discuss the relationship between Islam and peace. All these conferences concentrated on a defensive of Islam. It was useless. From some of the western states side, a new era in the world started to fabricate information. The phrase "axis of evil" appeared and included two Moslem states: Iraq and Iran. Many studies and actions sometimes provoke and hurt the feelings of Moslems. Some of the studies, like that of Samuel Huntington, highlight the elements of a clash between civilizations and pave the way for more hatred against Islam. Although that study looked at the civilizations as one unified one block of Latin America, Confucian, Hindu, Slavic Orthodox, African, and Japanese, the attack was on Islam only (Mumayez 2007). In the Arab and Moslem world, no such writings or actions attacking Christians, including the literature written after 11 September, exist. They were defensive studies to prove that Islam is a religion of forgiveness and tolerance. On an international level, no one listened to or cared for such studies by the Arabs or Moslem states.

At several times during different periods of history, there was a cold war between Islam and the west. Sometimes it erupts into open warfare, as happened during the Crusades. This time in the era of media, there was huge hysterical propaganda against Islam after September 11th.

What is New in My Study

This study is not like the studies which I mentioned above, which are defensive of the Moslem side or biased and attacking Islam from a western perspective. It concentrates on pure facts existing in Arab and Islamic history. This study will deal with the idea of RM. This expression relates to the early interest in human rights in the Arabian Peninsula before Islam. It relates to the job of the ultimate decision maker to achieve justice in his state. This job is practiced by the most powerful person in the government who can judge and carry out his orders. He is different from a lawyer or judge. The judge doesn't have the power to execute decisions.

Historically, the Arabs survived in the area which is known as the Middle East between two cultures who divided the area in the Mediterranean until the seventh century. There were the Persian and Roman Empires. The Eastern half of the Roman Empire appeared with Byzantium or Constantinople, the capital of the new empire Byzantine Empire, whose religion was Orthodox Christianity. There was a great struggle between the two empires and they weakened each other before peace was concluded in 602. In the south, the greater part of the Arabian Peninsula was inhabited by Arab tribes who had their own cultures. The most important cities were Mecca and Medina. In Mecca, they were idol worshippers. In Medina (which was called Yathrib), there were some Jews whose religion was Judaism. All the Arabs made a pilgrimage to Mecca to visit the holy temple every year. This small city was dominated by a tribe called Quraish, who had commercial business with Yemen, Syria, and Egypt. Islam appeared in this city in 610 and Mohammad the Apostle of God started his message in this city. The prophet left Mecca after twelve years, convincing 60 or 70 persons to become Moslems, and they immigrated to Medina. That marked the commencement of the Islamic Calendar. Ten years later, in 632, the prophet died. He was succeeded by Abu Bekr.

Historically the Arabs before and after Islam lived in the open desert—a hard life which required a man of outstanding characteristics. Such life made them more responsible. Moreover, they enjoyed the ideal of personal honor which prevented dishonorable actions, treachery, and ruthlessness.

Hilf El Fodhoul

The tribe of Quraish that ruled Mecca before Islam divided the functions of the state between the subtribes. This tribe that lived in Mecca was the dominant tribe of Arabia. She was rich and her economy depended on trade. The caravans of this tribe moved from the south of the Arabian Peninsula (Yemen) to Bilad El Sham (Syria). There is great commercial route between Damascus and Mecca. The holy Quran mentioned this trade and commercial movement in the winter and summer like this, since the Quraish have been united to fit out caravans' winter and summer:

> *Let them worship the Lord of this house. Quraish who enjoyed a great reputation in Trade enjoyed another reputation of having the Holy places. The House of God which attracts the Arabs to come for Mecca every year (Hajj). These things made Quraish committed to values and responsibility. All over the Islamic history Every ruler Caliphate who ruled in the Islamic World was from Quraish. All the rulers (Caliphates) came from Quraish for 600 years at least. No one darde to have the title (Caliphate) after the collapse of the Abbassi Empire. The Ottomans broke these traditions when Sultan Selim went to Mecca in 1525 and asked the Sherif of Mecca to pray for him in the Friday School Teaching. He the Sherif gave him more than he asked for and granted him the title, which the King of Saudia Arabia still uses; The Servant or the Guard of the Holy Shrines (Khadim El Harmain El Shareefain). Anyway Ib Khaldoun later gave very good explanation that Qurais doesn't mean blood necessarily, but Power (Asabieh).*

Quraish Concentration on Human Rights

Quraish concentrated on this aspect of human rights, and specifically on reducing or combating grievances, which is called RM. A famous story in history happened when a Yemenite merchant was robbed in the middle of the holy shrine. The men gathered and decided to help him get back what was robbed from him. They succeeded. So, they reached resolution and carried it out immediately. This was an informal court, but it achieved justice. The prophet was 25-year-old by then; he attended the meeting. He liked it and he encouraged to have it in Islam. This meeting was called Hilf El Fodhoul (Ibn Hesham). The word Hilf means an alliance, and El Fodhoul means the plural of El Fadhl and El Fadhl is the good thing.

The Islam Era

The Prophet was political and religious leader. He was a judge. After he died his successor was the Caliphate Abu Bekr. He was the first Caliphate after the prophet Mohammad. From the very beginning he addressed the people to assist him if he was in the right and criticize him if he was not (Ibn Hesham). Omar, the second Caliphate (634–644), was utterly dedicated to Islam. He was noted for his great justice. In RM, he had a very famous story when an Egyptian man complained to him that he had been beaten by the son of the governor (The Wali). Omar made his decision immediately and ordered the Egyptian to beat the son of the Governor (Hassan 1964). He addressed the Governor: "When did you enslave the people who were born free." This phrase is copied and mentioned in the first article of the Human Rights Declaration.

The Place

This kind of court is held in the mosque. Sometimes the Caliphate assigned specific hours for this purpose. Ali, the fourth Caliphate (656–661), assigned specific hours to meet people (Hassan 1964). The third Abbasid Caliphate, Mehedi (775–785), built a specific place like a Mosque with 4 doors. He called it Qubit El Mathalim (the place where grievants can complain to the Caliphate). He used to sit and wait for the grievants to come (Deawan means the Public Building). The Caliphate was very accessible (Massoudi 1986).

This place may be called Dewan El Mathalim. The person who supervises it is Sahib El Mathalim. His authority is above the authority of the judge (Hassan 111). It needs a strong man with a great image of authority and power to deter the aggressors. He does what the judge cannot do. He may investigate looking for clues, and he may postpone the decisions till everything is clarified. He may interfere and use his influence or power between the two parties to reach resolutions and reconcilement.

Usually, this role is practiced by the caliphate. In the early days of Islam, it was like that until the Caliphate El Mehedi took power. Sometimes he delegates. The Caliphate Ali delegates the power to his judge (Abi Edris El Khawlani). Other Caliphates did it like Muawiya (661–680), and Mutasim (833–842) (Massoudi 1986).

The Team

The Caliphate or the man whom he delegates were assisted by a team of five persons:

1. A judge to assist in understanding the law
2. Al Faqeeh an expert in understanding religion, Quran, and Sunnah
3. Guards who protects or arrest the aggressors
4. Writers for the sake of documentations
5. Witnesses who witness and who assist in information

The Cases and Subjects

The Caliphate or the man whom he delegates may see the following cases:

1. These grievances who complains about the government officials like governors and others
2. The cases of soldiers who don't have their rewards
3. The grievances who complain about the size of taxes
4. The cases of worshipping the God for example accusing any one of any case relates to his religion

Ibn Batouta, the famous Arab traveler who traveled through Asia and passed by India 800 years ago, wrote that he saw a king sitting to receive the grievances on two days, Mondays and Thursdays, to look into the stories of the grievants who complained. He was assisted by four men, who were sitting beside him. One was a prince. There were four doors, and at each door there was a prince. The person who wants to complain may submit the complaint to any one of them. If any of these princes did not receive the complaint, he may be punished by the King. The King used to sit and read all of the complaints for the rest of the day (Ibn Batouta 1967).

References

Ibn Khaldoun (Wali al Din Abdel Rahman b. Muhammad). Book One, The Prolegomena, Kitab al Ibar Wa Diwan Al Mubtada Wa l Khabar, prepared by Ibrahim Chabbouh and Ihsan Abbas (Tunis 2006).

Ibn Hesham (Abu Mohammad Abdi Malik bin Hesham Abd El malik El

Maafaari, El Ssereih El Nabawieh, 4 parts (Beruit Dar El geel, N.D.).

El Masoudi Abu Al hasan Ali bin Al hussein bin Ali, Morooj El Thahab wa Maadin El Jawher (Beruit Dar Al Kutb, 1986).

Hasan Ibrahim Hassan, *The Political, Religious, Cultural, and Social History of Islam* (Beruit Dar Al Andalus, 1986).

Ibn Batouta. *Rehalit Ibn Batouta*. Part One (Egypt,Cairo; El Maktaba El Tejarieh, 1967).

Ibrahim Mumayez, *Islam and the West Today and Yesterday in Political Islam Amman Message as a Model* (Zarka; Hashemite University, 2007).

CHAPTER 8

Between Politics and Literature: An Analysis of The Gift of Viziers by Abu-Mansour Al-Tha'alibi

In general, the book *Gift of Viziers* works on vizierate and viziers and whatever is related to them. The author, Abu-Mansour Al-Tha'alibi, has elaborated the viziers' affairs in detailed research. In particular, the author talked about:

- The origin of vizierate, its meaning and its derivations.
- The position of vizierate.
- The qualities of good viziers.
- The position of viziers among Arabs, Persians, and Indians.
- The kings' habits when appointing a vizier.
- The merits and benefits of vizierate.
- Experiences of other nations such as Greeks and Persians.
- The vizierate's good habits, rights, and supplies, and the king's rights to the vizier.
- Witticisms between kings and viziers.
- The vizierate's conditions and requirements.
- The vizierate's parts and forms.
- The qualities that a vizier should possess.
- The vizierate's kinds.
- The vizier's efficiency, jokes, praise, and forgiveness.
- Counseling.

Al-Tha'libi concentrated more than any other author on the vizierate's affairs through writing about the Islamic regime or administration. The excellence of this manuscript lies in the fact that it focused in particular on viziers and vizierates. It fills a gap in its subject since Al-Thalibi preceded others when he wrote comprehensively about viziers and vizierates.

It should be pointed out that Al-Tha'libi has a vast knowledge that enabled him to write on this topic. He left behind him a huge intellectual legacy (See the Al-Thalibi biography in the manuscript verification). It is not strange that Ibn–Khillikan "taken from Ibn- Bassam" described him by saying that Al-Thalibi was at the top of the authors of his time. He said, "He was the shepherd of the knowledge hills, the collector of the verse and prose sundries. He was the head of the authors of his time, judged by his peers as Imam of workbooks. His reputation was set as an example, to which people ride their camels. His Divans shone west and east as the stars shine in the darkness. His combinations are of the most famous positions and the most radiant sighting. No description, whether verse or prose, can fulfill their rights."[1]

His student, Ali Bin Al-Hassan Al-Bakhrazi, the author of "The Palace Doll," described him by saying "He is Naisabour's Jahez, the butter of ages and time, no eye has ever seen like him and no senior has ever denied his credit." He described his poetry as having pure prologues and nice imagery.

Abu-Mansour Al-Tha'alibi presented his ideas in a very exquisite way through five chapters (Babes):

- The first chapter is on the origin of vizierate, its meaning and derivation, the qualities of good viziers, the position of viziers among Arabs and Persians, and the habits of kings when appointing viziers.

- The second chapter is short, with no more than three pages, which describe the vizierate virtues and benefits and the viziers' position at the ruler.

- The third chapter consists of four sections along with an introduction about vizierate's good habits, rights and supplies.

- The forth chapter consists of nine sections about vizierates' divisions, forms, and the qualities that should be found in the vizier along with what has been previously mentioned of good habits and requirements.

- The fifth chapter works on competence, an overview of vizier's witticism, anecdotes, and beauty of words, along with the petitions to kings and viziers asking for forgiveness and consent. In addition, it includes some of the viziers' praises.

The manuscript is unique of its kind and is entitled to take a prominent place in the Arabic library. It is considered better than Niccolo Machiavelli's book *The Prince* for a reason that is connected with the ethics of this book, which *The Prince* lacks. Machiavelli had a purpose when he wrote the book: it was to pave the way for Cesare Borgia to unite and rule Italy.

I referred to the resources the author used to write his book whether they were proverbs or verse. As for the Holy Quran verses, I authenticated each verse as it appeared in the Holy Quran, I indicated the number of the verse and the name of the Surah in which it appeared. I also authenticated the Honored Hadiths of Prophet Muhammad "Peace be upon him." I also defined the eminent men and explained the ambiguous words.

At the beginning of each chapter I arranged contents for the chapter. I arranged the book material in the same way it originally appeared to maintain the subject sequence as mentioned by the author. In addition, I sought the help and consultation of some specialized people regarding the book's ideas.

This manuscript is preserved at the Egyptian House of Books (Dar al-Kutub). The film NO. is 188 and the manuscript number is 1,300. The number of papers is 44 with a measurement of 28 x18 cms. The number of the film at the University of Jordan is 354.603131324.

This book "The Gift of Viziers" is written by the Sheikh and Imam Abu Mansour Al-Tha'alibi, may Allah have mercy upon him and be pleased with him, Amin.[2]

(In the Name Of Allah the most beneficent, the most merciful; from whom we seek help. Praise is to the lord of the world, the God who created things with his mastered talent and wisdom. He executes destinies as he wills and he manages destinies with his ability. He created people in different kinds[3] and raised some of them above others in rank that some of them may take labor from others. And Allah hath favored some of you above others in provision, some being rich, others being poor but all were content with what Allah has divided. They submitted to Allah and followed him. He hath ordained for them that religion to follow in managing their affairs in a way that made people submit to their kings, viziers and leaders willingly or unwillingly In this management order went on giving a word to the ruling to be inevitable.)

Being Affected by a Real Vizier

Like Machiavelli, Al-Thalibi was influenced by a vizier. Machiavelli was affected by some ministers in a way that led him to write his book *The Prince*. Al-Tha'alibi was also influenced by a vizier. He says:

When I served our master the king of kings Khawarizm Shah,[4] he had an idea to serve his greatest vizier and ambassador Abu-Abdullah Al-Hamdouni by offering him this book.[5] He meant to solicit his grave talents and honors. He gave it the name of "The Gift of Viziers" (Tuhfat al-Wuzara'), and arranged it into five chapters.[6]

The First Chapter

The first chapter works on the origin of the vizierate and its derivation. Our Lord Allah tells in the Holy Quran about prophet Moses who pleaded God by saying

> "Appoint for me a vizier from my folk, Aaron, my brother. Confirm my strength with him. And let him share my task, that we may glorify Thee much. And much remember Thee. Lo! Thou art ever seeing us. He said: Thou art granted thy request, O Moses." (Taha, 25-36)

Aaron was the first one to be appointed as a vizier. He took the place of his brother in achieving many of Bani Israel missions. More than that, he took Moses' place when Moses went out to meet Allah in the appointed tryst.

Kings of Persia, Greece, and India used to adopt viziers for their countries. They had their own situations, laws, and features written in their own languages. The word vizier is derived from the Arabic word, "wizr," which means "burden" because viziers carry the burden of work instead of their kings. Our Lord Allah said,

> "But we were laden with burdens of ornaments of the folk" (Taha, 87). Allah also said,"Till the war lay down its burdens" (Muhammed, 4). This means putting down weapons, because fighters wear heavy weapons which burden them. Al-Asha says,[7] "I prepared for the war its burdens, Long spears and stags, and what David has woven Camel footwear that is heard one after the other."

It is said that the word is driven from assistance since the vizier assists the king in bearing the burden of policy. Our lord Allah says, "Appoint for me a vizier from my folk, Aaron, my brother. Confirm my strength with him" (Taha, 29-31). This means that having a vizier makes him stronger because he helps and assists him. Allah says, "We will strengthen thine arm with thy brother" (Al-Qasas, 35). "as sown corn that sendeth forth its shoot and strengtheneth it" (AlFath, 29). Shoot means the small plants that grow around the stem. Strengthen means helpd him with his little kids and checks.

It is said that the word is of Persian origin and later on it was introduced into Arabic. It is taken from zawar), which is a name they use for strength and intensity. It is borrowed and introduced into Arabic with the meaning of strengthening the country's owner and helping in executing the mission he is about to execute. Apparently, the word means assistance and help. Aisha (may Allah be pleased with her) said:

> "If Allah wants to do someone something good (or she said if Allah wants to do a prince something good) he would send him an honest vizier. If he remembers he helps him. If he forgets he reminds him. If Allah wants something else, he sends him a dishonest vizier. If he forgets the vizier doesn't remind him. If he remembers, the vizier doesn't help him."[8]

The Importance of Viziers among Civilizations

Al-Tha'alibi reviewed the importance of viziers at Persian, Indian, and Greek nations in addition to their kinds and qualities at the Arab nations. As for selecting viziers, the Persian kings kept on selecting their viziers and counselors. The least king had at least three viziers with the number reaching up to 17 viziers. Indian kings also say that a king should have at least four viziers. Greek and Nabatean, Roman, and Frank kings were never without a vizier or a counselor.

Anushirawan used to say, "'The most informative king can't do without a vizier exactly as the best swords that can't do without being polished, and the animals that can't do without the whip and the wisest women who can't do without a husband."

Because the viziers have a high position at the prince's councils since they share them in carrying out different tasks and in managing their affairs, the proverb went on saying, "Don't be conceited by the prince if you were cheated by the vizier."

In the same meaning, Abul-Fadl Bin Al-Amid told his friend from the Alawite who was specialized in working with Rukn Adwala:

> "You claimed that you are not thinking after you had become under the protection of the Prince.
>
> Be gone your mistaken idea which gave the illusion that you can do without the vizier
>
> Skies can't go without earth as well as earth can't do without the sky."[9]

And in the couplet known as "That al –Holal":

> "If you seek to get something from the Prince
> You have to approach him through the vizier"

What a beautiful line Abu Tammam said to Muhammed Bin Abdel-Malek the vizier of Al-Mu'tasem and Al-Watheq: "Hey Abu Ja'afar if the caliph wants us to be the sea, you will then be the coast."

Depending on this meaning, Yahia Bin Ali Bin Yahia the Astrologer said The Prince of the Faithful is a full sea with a surpassing generosityAbul-Najm, for those who seek him, is the door that leads to this sea.

The Importance of Religion

Al-Tha'alibi mentions the narration of Abul-Fath Al-Besti, who praised a vizier but hesitated to describe him as the wisest vizier because of his religion. He said, "One day Abul-Fath Al-Besti told me, 'I haven't known until yesterday that the Sabi Abu-Isaaq is the most eloquent and best writer. If it wasn't for his religion, I would say he is the wisest. I have found a part of his speech about God's wisdom in making people of different classes and their need for kings and viziers and their need for each other and that this arrangement makes the world better. I was driven crazy by his words and even envied him for such thinking.'"

Viziers and Age

It became clear that appointing elderly people who were knowledgeable and experienced as viziers was more important than appointing young people. Al-Tha'alibi said, "I read about Mosa Bin Abdel-Malek who said that Al-Fadl Bin Abbas distributed some of his counselors as spies for all over the states. He ordered them to inquire about his imperfections. One of these spies came back and told him that a group of people came to Al-Ma'moun and when they went out, they said that they had never seen such a king in his mind and his majesty, and that they had never seen an efficient vizier as his vizier except that he was young. It was kings' habits to appoint Sheikhs (elders) as viziers since they add experience to knowledge and cleverness to presidency. Al-Fadl disappeared for three days working on dying his beard until it became white."

The Good Vizier

Al-Tha'alibi elaborated in concentrating on the good vizier: his origin and eloquence, his morals, his management and his human soul that enjoins him to do good or to do bad. In addition to appointing reputable nobles as viziers and not appointing unknown persons with humble reputation. Appointing humble people as viziers exposes the kingdom to be lost exactly as had happened with Izz-Al-Dawlah Bukhtiar who appointed the master of his kitchen Abu Taher Muhammed Bin Baqqeya as a vizier. The man became a joke among the people of lower classes, "From the plate to the vizierate" (Mena al-ghadara ela elwizara), it is said. Al-Tha'alibi said that prophet Muhammad "Peace be upon him" said,

> "If Allah wants to do a king something good, he would send
> him an honest vizier. If he forgets he reminds him. If he
> intends to do something good he helps him, and if he sets
> out to do something bad, he stops him."

All opinions had met that a king's vizier should possess origin and eloquence, conclusive words, good habits, insightful opinion, and the right arrangement. He must refer to a soul that enjoins him to do good away from evil, with deliberation on the paths of righteousness. He should also combiner the tools of sovereignty along with the equipment of presidency all of which is accompanied with comprehensive love for the public and the private. He spends his days between counseling, working hard for the interest of the kingdom and bearing the responsibility of getting closer to his Sultan. His excellence and criticism are as pure as gold. If a virtuous king meets a good counseling vizier, you know that the kingdom will become calm and tranquil with all its affairs going on promptly with safe trade routes, low prices, and the gaps of virtue smiling, and the souls of the folks placid in the shades of tranquility, enjoying themselves in the security gardens.

The pillar of the matter in every vizierate is to appoint reputable nobles as viziers and not to qualify unknown persons with humble reputation as more than one king did, which caused them to earn bloodshed and destruction of their policy's corners exactly as had happened with Izz-Al-Dawlah Bukhtiar.[11]

Being Excluded to One Vizier

Al-Tha'alibi connected between the perils a state may be exposed to and the large number of viziers. In the past, there was no Ministers Council presided by a Prime Minister as we have nowadays. The vizier plays the role of a counselor. He comes second after the king. Al-Tha'alibi says that it was the kings' habits to appoint one, two, or more viziers. This is unwise and shows fault in management since it exposes the kingdom to perils. A sheath can't hold more than one sword, and having more than one repairing hand causes matters to be spoilt. The old saying went: "Having more than one navigator causes the ship to sink."

Abbasid Caliphs, although their kingdom was wide extending from the east to the west adopted the habit of appointing just one vizier as we are told by history books. It wasn't until the late days of Al-Muqtader that the states' policy weakened. The Vizier Ali Bin Issa was fired,[12] although he was merited with virtue, justice, rectitude, and steadfastness, and was replaced by Hamid Bin Al-Abbas despite his deficiency and failure.

Afterwards, they couldn't do without Ali because he was efficient and capable of doing what others couldn't do. He joined Hamid and he was assigned to follow up the Divans. They both shared the vizierate. While Hamid won the fame, Ali did most of the work until it was said "Abu Ali Simjor[13] was defeated because he had many viziers with opposing counseling in which one spoils what the other repairs until it ended to the worst consequences with the ugliest fates."

The Vizierate's Virtues and Benefits

Al-Tha'alibi praises the benefits of vizierates and reviews the experiences of the Persians and Greeks. Our Lord Allah says in the Holy Quran:

> "We verily gave Moses the Scripture and placed with him
> his brother Aaron as vizier (Al-Furqan, 35).

This came as a gratitude in answering what Prophet Moses asked for:

"Appoint for me a vizier from my folk, Aaron, my brother. Confirm my strength with him" (Taha, 29-32).

The vizier is a kind of support and back up who manages the affairs of the king. It is narrated about Prophet Muhammed "Peace be upon him" saying,

"If Allah wants to do a prince something good, he would send him a good vizier" or an honest vizier. If he remembers he helps him. If he forgets he reminds him. If Allah wants something bad, or he said something else, he sends him a dishonest vizier. If he forgets the vizier doesn't remind him. If he remembers, the vizier doesn't help him."

Khosrau Kavadh said that a vizier is the king's sight, hearing, heart, and mind. His doors are locked, and he is out of sight. He should be conserved and noticed. He should conserve the state's interests and keep it well-organized and beautiful, since he keeps away any casual lesion that may lead to the state's corruption. The vizier is like a skilful doctor who cares about conserving people's health and healing any ailment the body suffers from.

Al-Fadl Bin Sahl said: "The just king with the virtuous vizier is like a great river with an easy course, and the good king with a bad vizier is like a sweet pure river full of crocodiles that rarely benefit any one. They are also like a ripe garden with a lion living in it."[14]

Aristotle said, "Alexander elected seven viziers to accompany him in his travels to handle his interests and affairs. He told them the following: 'The king had shared you his kingdom, make this blessings last by offering him advice, raise the pillars of the kingdom, fix its bases, fortify it with justice, decorate it with virtue, repair the defects before you become unable to fix them, cease the opportunity before it gets too late. Anyway, you are the king's partners. If you win him you win, if you lose him you lose. Work for yourselves and for others. May God bless you.'"

The Vizierate's Good Habits, Rights, and Provisions

Al-Tha'alibi mentioned the following about the viziers' good habits, rights, and provisions.

The person who is selected to be a vizier should combine good manners, mature deeds, rectitude, good management, right and useful opinions. In this way, he can be just, honest, brave, and diplomatic. At the time of peace and truce, it is good for the vizier to be calm and forbearing. At the time of wars and disorders, it is good for the vizier to be brave and firm. Some virtuous men said that the requirements of vizierate are five:

The First:

Justice, To be fair in his judgment where people are safe from his (and others') injustice.

The Second:

Honesty, Paying what he owes to others, and to get his due rights from others, and to store money for himself. Thus his workers get glad with his way of life.

The Third:

Competence, The knowledge of the worldly actions and behaviors, and the money investments and extractions. He puts things in their right place and orders actions according to their bases.

The Fourth:

Diplomacy, knowing how to win the love and admiration of the soldiers and how to attune their hearts, how to gather or disperse them, and to be an expert in war machinations and deceptions. To keep the state's borders, fortresses, gabs, and borders safe.

The Fifth:

To combine harshness with kindness, being harsh on strong ones until they relent, and being kind with the weak until they gets fair treatment. In this way, the vizier is bold and fearless if he is forced to face horrors. He refrains from taking decisions if he is denied the right opinions. Some poets pointed to some viziers who were appointed without having these qualities by saying:

> "No competence, no beauty
> No eloquence no articulation

You are just a portrait

Where are the vizier's qualities?"

Some poets praised the Vizier Abu-Nasr Al-Otabi by saying: "God had gathered in the vizier virtues that are above destinies."[16]

Abu Zaid Al-Balkhi said, describing the perfect vizier, that he should combine "virtuous qualities along with good morals where joviality gathers with grouper, forbearance, prestige, courage, and persistence in order to be able to put things straight. Other qualities should be added such as chastity, honesty, and self-esteem, knowledge of writing and its controls, good statements, knowledge of the life and news of the past in a way that benefits in his being informed of their experiments and returns. He should also be good looking with acceptable image. If he were over forty years of age, it would be better for him to become wiser and more experienced."[17]

Others said, "A virtuous vizier should have a nice guise with dignity. He should be silenced by forbearance, articulated by science, with good handwriting, eloquence in brevity and articulation that make them approach their purpose along with being cautious in correspondence, all of which originates from religion, honesty and chastity."

He also said, "The most harmful thing for kings is to appoint viziers who are good at words with no deeds. When the kings rely on such viziers' speech their kingdom is caused to fall apart because of the viziers' negligence or bad actions."

A wise man said, "If you see that a vizier collects money to himself, dismiss him. There is no good in him because the love of money gets over his mind and prevents him from following up the kingdom's interests. If you see that a vizier loves fame and reputation for himself while neglecting the kingdom's affairs, there is no good in him because his infidelity to the king's grace caused him to gain this fame."

Khasraus used to require that viziers should have sound senses, sound organs, beautiful image along with what was mentioned before of mind, opinion, dignity, poise, and others. If he added to this good handwriting and good speech with knowledge of areas, geometry, arithmetic, good conduct in political affairs and royal management, being informed of the early nations' history and experience, being truthful in speech with high spirits, honest, not being envious, irascible, bored, conceited, greedy, drunkard, laughing or forgetful, the requirements of the vizierate are complete in him and thus he becomes fit to manage the kingdoms' affairs.

A Description of the Prince or the Vizier

We present here an excellent description of the prince or vizier's character:

> What is meant by a vizier the man who helps the first man in the state. Amr Bin Mesa'dah[18] wrote:-"I sought for my affairs a man that combines virtue, good manners along with straightforwardness. Good manners had seasoned him. Experiments had made him wise. If you tell him a secret he keeps it. He is capable of achieving any task assigned to him. He is silenced by forbearance and articulated by science. He is satisfied with an instant and can do by a hint. He has the prince's authority, the Wiseman's patience, the scientists' humbleness, and the writers' understanding. He catches men's heart with his sweet words. The Virtuous are stunned by his eloquence. His gentle kindness makes him live in people's heart. If someone does him good he thanks him and if he is afflicted by offence he waits in patience and consideration. This is the kind of man that the public affairs should be delegated to.

Abul-Fath Al-Sabti said about Al-Saheb Bin Abbad:[19]

> "A young man who combined the perches of knowledge, chaste, sturdiness, and generosity beyond compare. Exactly like apples having combined beauty, elegance, sweet fragrance and taste."

The Vizier's Duties Towards the King

Al-Tha'alibi mentioned the vizier's duties towards the king as follows:

> The vizier should be committed with the following rights to the king: Faithfulness in counseling, making their efforts to keep the kingdom sound, safe and away from scourge. This can be elaborated through various rights. Some of these rights are desirable, others are imperative. First of all, being loyal in counseling and amiability without hav-

ing inner deception, and not sparing him his money or his soul without upholding an enemy against him or hiding a piece of advice the king needs to be informed about.

Other rights include exposing the king's concealed advantages, referring good deeds to him, concealing his bad deeds even if they are mentioned, and keeping track of whoever says otherwise about the king until he removes it out either by oppression or by kindness.

Other rights include being humble in front of him, respecting him in his presence and in his absence. It is said that the more your king honors you, the more humble you should be. He should not match him with beauty, delicacy, residence, riding, clothing, servants, or footnotes. If he perceived that the king has a liking for something the vizier owns, he should give it up to him.

This also includes carrying out his orders after reconsidering them: if he saw something wrong, or if he feared something hateful, he should correct it and remove the imperfection. Good habits indicate that first of all he should listen and obey, but he should try to prevent carrying the order until he meets the king in privacy and revises the order with him. If he couldn't do so, he then should write to the king to clarify his point of view regarding the imperfection that he fears. Afterwards, he works in accordance with the king's decision and agreement. This includes following up the construction of cities, repairing the defects, investing money in cultivating plants, procuring the construction requirements and encouraging people to build up the state, since building up increases money, and with money kingdoms get higher with plentiful assistants.

Al-Tha'alibi wrote a chapter about the qualities that should be found in this vizier in addition to what has been mentioned above of requirements and good habits:

> The vizier needs to combine Islam, maturity (adulthood) and mind along with the terms of justice. As for freedom, it has not been agreed upon. What is right is that it is not one of the terms as required to be a king or an Imam of prayers. In addition, he needs to be described as having a wise mind, good opinions, knowledge of policy, and not to be dazzled by things no matter how great they are, and not to be surprised by views and actions if they get plen-

tiful. He should be persistent, grave, rising, executive and deciding.

The poet says:

> "His ideas and wit are the same when things get mingled for people
>
> He shows the firmest opinions just when the counselors get confused."[20]

Such vizier has the right to be taken care of, not to be dismissed as long as he doesn't commit a misdemeanor or treason.

Such vizierate is general and complete. Its vizier should take care of all its affairs from the tiniest to the greatest. He should appoint fit magistrates (Walis). Meanwhile he should carry out tours of inspections through which he checks out their conditions where he acknowledges the sufficient, enlightens the stupid, teaches the ignorant, punishes the traitor and dismisses the inefficient.

This vizier should cast a close look at the tiniest interests of the kingdom in order to improve it and make it strong and immune. He should spread out his spies to collect the news without neglecting any imperfection or corruption that may appear to threaten the kingdom. In the past, a wise man said: "Don't tolerate a small thing that may potentially increase." The vizier should not hide any of these events from the king. This meaning is collected in the verse written by Nasr Bin Sayar the Wali (magistrate) of Khurasan which he wrote to Marwan when Abu-Muslim appeared:[21]

> "I see a spark through the ashes that are about to ablaze
>
> Two stones make fire ablaze
>
> While wars breakout with words
>
> If you don't put it out
>
> War will break out
>
> With people and palaces as its fuel
>
> I say I wish I knew
>
> Are Bani Umayyah awake or asleep?"

The Vizier's right to the King can be summarized as follows:

1. To raise their esteem.

2. Not to listen to informers because the vizier is meant and envied. A Persian wise man summarized this by saying, "Not to blame without a proven right, not to forward someone who is below him in writing, and not to empower his enemy on him."

Counseling

Al-Tha'alibi elaborated in writing about counseling. He said,

> Our God Allah said while teaching the profit (Peace be upon him),
>
> "and consult them in affairs (of moment). Then, when thou hast taken a decision put thy trust in Allah" (Al-Emran, 159).
>
> Our prophet Mohammed "Peace be upon him" said,
>
> "He who seeks consultation will not be disappointed, and he who asks for guidance will not repent it."[22]

He also said "The consulted is a trusted advisor,"[23] by which he means that advice should be offered to those who ask for it, and they should keep the trust for those who seek counseling.

Through counseling policy is managed and opinions are exchanged. The policy is the country's system and the kingdom's picture. If this requirement weakens or spoils, the kingdom is weakened and spoiled. Some scientists said "Opinions are the measurement of future matters on similar past matters. The opinions' substance is the direct experiments that are witnessed or heard of. Elderly people are preferred to be counseled because they came through a lot of experiments. Young people can be consulted on the condition that they posses correct mood, sound talent, and plentiful sciences and narrations.

Al-Ma'moun recommended his son while teaching him to consult those who posses opinion, experience, and cleverness because they know better of time changeability and matters' management. Therefore, you have to obey them and to bear their harshness since they disclose the defects in order to arrive to the hoped for amendment. He who gives you the medicine so that you may get better is far better than the one who feeds you with sweet things that cause you to be ill.

The poet says:

> "He who is careful may attain some of his needs
> He who is in a hurry may commit mistakes."[24]

The Judge Al-Jarjani (May Allah bless his soul) said,

> "Consult others if a disaster one day befalls you
> Even though your counseling is usually sought
> The eye meets far and near struggle
> But it can't see itself except through a mirror."

In our heritage it is said:

> "When you consult rational people you become rational
> When you disobey them you will repent it."

It is also said, "The person who seeks counseling will be praised if he does the right thing, and will be excused if he makes mistakes."

Some scientists said, "Counseling and opinions are pure psychological industry. Because of that, it is mostly honored. On the other hand, carrying things on the head or on any other part of the body is a physical industry. Because of that, it is mostly contemptuous. Committing mistakes in this respect is extremely harmful. A lot of blood was shed, many countries were destroyed, incest were violated because of the bad and faulty opinions. Some wise sayings state,

> "Consult before you indulge, be empowered before you repent." A vizier, when encountered by a calamity, should be steady in counseling, leaven opinions without being hasty. Carefulness and deliberation increases the easiness of difficult things and the insightfulness of ideas. He should renew consultation after being deliberate since some evils have inconstant signs with no origin. There is no good in hasty opinions.

Consultation

In this chapter, Al-Tha'alibi elaborated in describing who should be consulted and who shouldn't.

He said, "You should select people of abundant knowledge, numerous experience and sober solutions." Al-Balkhi said, "Consult that who has experience, and who was tossed and preceded by accidents unless he is weakened or changed by old age or illness." He continued, "At war time, scientists of sound minds, not people of war are consulted. I read a letter written by Abdullah Bin Hamza Al-Alawi Al- Najem[26] at Yemen, in which he wrote that consulted people should combine four things: religion, mind, advice, and affection. Whoever lacks such traits is considered a hidden disease.

"If you are in need to send a messenger

Send a wise man and don't commend him

If a counselor approaches you one day,

Don't depart him or keep him away

If you are puzzled by a certain matter,

Consult a clever man and don't disobey him."

Some virtuous men said, "Don't consult those who mean to win your approval to satisfy your inclinations, or who rely on disagreeing with you to deviate from you. Depend on those who seek the right whether with you or against you."

It was said, "He who seeks approval and permission from their brothers is a cheater and traitor. The person who does this in Fiqh will issue wrong Sharia' rulings, and who does this in medicine will increase ailments."

This was the case of Al-Muqtader State.[27] The state suffered from weakness, decay and disrupted management. The kingdom's foundations were corrupt. The reason that can't be concealed is that he became caliph when he was too young. His mother, his aunt and the housekeeper took the controls of managing the kingdom's affairs which lead to this bad situation. Rarely do women or young children possess mindful thinking and opinions.

Al-Tha'alibi mentioned that competent people are those who combine eloquence with politics. They pass fair judgments, pronounce final decisions, they bear the responsibility of the state, manage the kingdom's affairs, and handle the public. If you add to a vizier's eloquence, good handwriting, beautiful appearance, stratagem in policy, sound ideas, stability and determination, he would, in this way, be credited with his knowledge and considered fit for managing the states and kingdoms.

Arabs are known for their eloquence and assonance of which they are usually proud. The Arab is also known of their affectation of courtesy. There was a group of the Umayyad kings and Walis (magistrates) who were known for possessing rhetoric, diplomacy, and prudence. We mention here some of them without the requirement of advancement or delay:

- Amr Bin Al-Ass, he was famous for his cunning, policy , and managing wars and states. He was Mu'aweya's vizier and counselor.
- Ziad Bin Sumayya who is claimed to be descendant of Abu-Sufian. He was known for his eloquent orations, brief and eloquent letters, famous policy, and control of actions.
- Al-Hajjaj Bin Yousuf Al-Thaqafi was eloquent and capable of rhetoric, strict policy and firmness in management. His excessive injustice, tyranny, recklessness had moved him from being a virtuous politic into being a wretched one.

There are other viziers and writers who were competent and eloquent such as:

Qubaisa Bin Thuwayb,[28] Raja' Bin Haiwa Al-Kindi,[29] Amr Bin Habira,[30] Abdel Hamid Bin Yahia.[31]

As for Al- Abbasids, the Person who called for establishing the state is Abu Muslem Abdel-Rahman bin Muslim Al-Khurasani who was a man of policy, endeavor, and eloquence.

The Abbasid caliphs were eloquent with policy and management such as Al-Mansour, Al-Mahdi who managed all his affairs by himself, Al-Rashid, Al-Ma'moun who is considered Bani Abass's scientist, Al-Mu'tasem, their diplomatic, Al-Mu'taded and others.

Until now, their children are still caliphs known for their knowledge and virtue. The Abbasid state had innumerable number of eloquent and competent viziers and walis (magistrates) such as Abu-Salamah Al-Khallal,[32] who was the first to be called vizier, and all the Barmak family specially Ja'far bin Yahia. Barmak family's origin goes back to the son of Barmak who was honoured by Persians and was a follower of their religion. They ended up by being eloquent in Arabic, and mastering all arts of writing. Some people made up some stories and petitions which they raised to Ja'far for the purpose of getting his signature on their patches. There was also Al-Fadl Bin Sahl who was titled "Thul-Re'asatayn" (the man with two commands) and his brother Al-Hasan, who were Persians too. There was also Al-Fath bin Khaqan and his son, Amr bin Mesa'dah, and Muhammad bin Abdelmalek Al-Zayyat who was unjust in nature.

Conclusion

Any king will never arrive to what he aims to of good management and control unless he receives good assistance from viziers and assistants who carry out actions.

Any benefit from a vizier would not be complete unless he had complemented such qualities as knowledge of the actions they manage, good policy, considering its forms and rules, with access to knowing its careers and mystiques, being faithful in advising the king in a way that makes the king prefers him to himself and to all other people, and to be deeply in love with him. If he were so, without wasting rights or seeking it intending to cheat the king, and without taking any defect in the kingdom's affairs lightly, not seeking prestige through approving what the king desires although it might seem harmful, refraining from stealing money, sensing what may lead to a waste of an action or derogation of right, and assigning to his family, assistants, and bodyguards whatever he assigns to himself.

It is also said that only qualified people can bear the burden of vizierate. Everyone aspires to become a vizier since he has the place of hearing, sight, tongue and heart of the king. Don't you see that the king is invisible from people and that his door is closed for the public? And that whatever he orders he needs his vizier to execute his orders, to know whether he lies or he tells the truth, he also needs him to keep his money and treasures lest someone deceives him. For any piece of news no matter how far it is, or any event hidden or kept by workers and walis, the king needs the vizier to report it to him and to express his opinion about it.

Notes

1. Ibn Khallikan 1:291. See also his book (Themar Al-Quloub Fel-Mudaf wal-Mansoub), verified by Abul-Fadl Ibrahim (Cairo, Dar el-Ma'aref, 1985).

2. The author Abu Mansour Tha'ālibī (961–1038) (329-350). Abdul-Malik ibn Mahommed ibn Isma'il Abu Mansour Al- Tha'alibi, was born in Nishapur, Iran. He worked on literature and became Imam of literature and languge. He wrote many books such as: Yatimat Al-Dahr 4 volumes, Al-Latae'f wal-Zarae'f, Fiqh Al-Lugha, Yawaqit Al-Mawaqit, Sehr Al-Balagha, Al-Muntahal, Lata'ef Al-Ma'aref, Al-Mubhej, Ghurar Akhbar Al-Furs, Bard Al-Akbad, He Who missed the Singer, Al-Amthal, What has happened between Al-Mutanabi and Saif Al-Dawala, Khass Al-Khass, Nathr Al-Nazm wa Hal Al-Oqad, Makarem Al-Akhlaq, Themar Al-Quloub fi Al-Mudaf wal Mansoub, Ser Al-Adab, Al-Kenaya wal–Ta'reedh "Al-Nehaya fel-Kenaya, Al-Mo'nes Al-Waheed, Mera't Al-Murwat, Ahsan Ma Sam'et.

   He also wrote some manuscripts such as: Tuhfat Al-Wuzra', Ghurar Al-Balagha, Ahsan Al-Mahasen, Al-Ghelman, Al-Tjnees, Tabaqat Al-Molouk, Al-Mutashabeh (a letter), Al-Tamthil wal-Muhadara, Al-Shakwa wal-Itab, Al-Maqsour wal-Mamdoud.

3. This word means different. (The dictionary of "Maqyees Al-Lugha," Ibn Fares 234\2).

4. He was mentioned in Al-Tha'alibi book "Nathr Al-Nazm wa Hal Al-Oqad (Beirut, Dar Al-Rae'd Al-Arabi, 1983), p. 2. He is Abul-Abbas Ma'moun Bin Ma'moun Khawarism Shah. See *The History of Abul-Fadl Al-Bayhaqi*, p. 734.

5. Abu-Abdallah Al-Hamdouni, the vizier of Abul-Abbas Ma'moun Bin Ma'moun Khawarism Shah whom Al-Tha'alibi mentioned in other books such as Nathr Al-Nazm wa Hal Al-Oqad, Al-Kenaya wal-Ta'rid. It is noticed that Al-Tha'alibi gave him the title of the Great Vizier, The Most Prestigious Vizier.

6. Malek Al-Zaman Vizier Abu-Abdalla Al-Hamdouni is addressed here. The book is divided in the same way that Al-Tha'alibi divides his other books. This wipes out any doubt regarding ascribing the manuscript to Al-Tha'alibi.

7. His Divan, p. 149. The second line's narration goes as follows: "and from what David had woven shields on caravans one following the other."

8. Hadith Sahih narrated by Abu-Daoud (2932), Al-Baihaqi 10\111-112, corrected by Ibn-Habban (44949).

9. See Al-Tha'alibi""Yatimat Al-Dahr"" 04-203\3.

10. Abu-Abdalla Muhammed Bin Abdous Al-Koofi, known as AL-Jahshyari. He is one of those who wrote about viziers. He has a book called "Kitab AL-Wuzra". Al-Tha'alibi mentioned that book.

11. Bukhtiar Abu–Mansour Izz Adawlah Ibn Mu'ez Adawlah Ahmed Bin Boyed (942–978) (331-367) was a famous poet who was known for his strength and intense sturdity. He became a Sultan after his father. His cousin Adudh Adawla killed him. See Al-Zarkali-Al-Alam Volume 2, p. 11.

12. Vizier Ali Bin Issa Bin Daoud Bin Al-Jarrah Abul-Hasan Al-Baghdadi Al-Husni (859–946) (244-334). He was vizier of Al-Muqtader and Al-Qaher. He lived a troubled life. He died in Baghdad. He has an anthology called "Divan Al-Rasa'el" and "Ma'ani Al-Qur'an" which Ibn Mujahed the recitor (Muqri') assisted him to write. He also wrote the books "Jame' Al-Dua,'" "Kitab Al-Kitab," and "Seirat Al-Khulafa." See Al-Zarkali-Al-Alam Volume 5, pp. 133-134.

13. Abu-Ali Seimajor is a Samanid Prince.

14. Al-Fadl Bin Sahl Al-Sarkhi (771–818) (154-202) is Al-Ma'moun's vizier. He was majusi but converted to Islam through Al-Ma'moun. He was titled "Thol-Rea'satyn" (The Man with Two Commands) because he was in command of the vizierate and the army. It was claimed that Al-Ma'moun poisoned him. He died in Sarkhas where he was born. (See Al-Zarkali-Al-Alam, Volume 5, p. 354).

15. Nezam Al-Malek Ali Bin Isaaq (1018–1092) (408-485). He is Abul-Hasan Bin Ali Bin Isa'q Al-Tousi from Tus. He was the vizier of Alp Arslan and Malek Shah. (See Al-Zarkali-Al-Alam Volume 2, p. 219).

16. Abu-Nasr Al-Atbi (1036) (427) from Al-Ray. He grew up in Khorasan. He is a poet and a historian. (See Al-Zarkali-Al-Alam Volume 7, p. 156).

17. Abu-Zaid Al-Balkhi (849–934) (235-322). He is Ahmed Bin Sahl Al-Balkhi. He was born and died in Balakh. He was an unequaled scientist. His books, which were mentioned in Ibn-Al-Nadim book "El-Fehrest," "The Index," reflected that he was well-informed. Some of his books are "Kitab Al-Seyasah Al-Kabir," "Kitab Al-Seyasah Al-Saghir," "Kitab Al-Shataranj," "Fadae'l Balakh," "Adab Al-Sultan Warae'ya," "Akhlaq Al-Omam;" the book "Kitab

Al-Bede' Wattarikh" is ascribed to him. (See Al-Zarkali-Al-Alam Volume 5, p. 131).

18. Amr Bin Mesa'dah Bin Sa'ad Bin Soul Abul-Fadl Al-Souli is one of Al-Ma'moun viziers. He was an eloquent writer. He died in Adana, Turkey. (See Al-Zarkali-Al-Alam Volume 5, p. 260.)

19. Al-Sahib Bin Abbad (938–955) (326-385). He is Ismae'l Bin Abbad Bin Al-Abbas Abul-Qasem Al-Talqani. He was the vizier of Mua'yyad Adawlah bin Boyid and his brother Fakhr Adawla. He was born in Al-Talqan at Qazween and died in Asfahan. (See Al-Zarkali-Al-Alam Volume 1, p. 313).

20. It is mentioned in the book "Al-Ahkam Al-Sultaneyyeh," "The Ordinance of the Government." If these qualities are complete in a leader, reform would be general from his point of view. See Abul-Hasan Ali Bin Muhammed Bin Habib Al-Basri Al-Baghdadi Al-Mawardi (450, hijrah). "Al-Ahkam Al-Sultania" "The Ordinance of the Government" (Beirut, Dar el-Kutub Al-Elmeyyah, p. 26).

21. Nasr Bin Siar Rafe' Bin Harey Bin Rabia'h Al-Kinani (748-131 hijrah). He is Mudhar's Sheikh at Khurasan and wali of Balakh and then Kurasan. The call of Abbasids was strengthened at his time. Al-Tarmanin, pp. 824-825.

22. Verified by Al-Tabrani in "Al-Mu'jam Al-Saghir," p. 204. Al-Haithami said in "Majma' Al-Zawae'd" 8\96 that it was narrated by Al-Tabarani in "Al-Awsat" and "Al-Saghir," through Abdesalam Bin Abdel-Qudous. It is very weak.

23. Verified by Abu-Daoud (5128) and Al-Tarmazi (2822), and Ibn-Majah (3745) through Abu-Hurairah.

24. Omair Bin Shuyyem Bin Amr Bin Abbad from Bani Jasham Bin Bakr Abu said Al-Taghlibi who was titled Al-Qattami. He was a Christian from Taghlib, Iraq. He was known as Sari' Al-Gawani. (See Al-Zarkali-Al-Alam Volume 5, p. 264.)

25. Al-Qadhi Al-Jarjani. He is Ahmed Bin Ahmed Bin Al-Abbas AlJarjani (1089-482 hejrah). He is the judge of Basra and Shafe' Sheikh. His books include: Al-Tahrir, Al-Bulgha, Al-Shafi, and Al-Mua'yah. (See Al-Zarkali-Al-Alam Volume 1, p. 207.)

26. Abdullah Bin Hamzah Al-Alawi (1161–1217) (561-614 hejrah). He is one of the Zaideyyah Imams, scientist and poet. (See Al-Zarkali-Al-Alam Volume 4, p. 213.)

27. Al-Muqtader Bellah (895–932) (282-320 hejrah). He is Ja'afar Bin Ahmed

Bin Talha Abul-Fadl, Al-Muqtader Bellah Bin Al-Mu'taded Ibn Al-Muwa-faq. He was born in Baghdad, and proclaimed a caliph in 295. After a year he was thrown down then he was proclaimed again. His main assistant was his servant Mu'nes who came out with armored force against him. He defeated the caliph and killed him. (See Al-Zarkali-Al-Alam Volume 2, p. 115.)

28. Qubaisah Bin Thuwa'ib Al-Khuza'i Al-Madani. He died in (705-86 hejrah). He was born in the year of Conquest. (A'm Al-Fath). He was a trusted narrator of Hadith from Al-Madina. He contacted Abdel-Malek Bin Marwan. He died in Damascus. (Al-Tarmanini, p. 605.)

29. Raja' Bin Haiwah Bn Jarwal Al-Kindi Abul-Meqdaam Abu Nasr (731-112 hejrah). He was a scientist and eloquent. He accompanied Omar Bin Abdel-Aziz when he was a prince. (Al-Tarmanini, p. 712.)

30. Amr Bin Habirah Bin Sa'ad Bin Odai Al-Fazazi (728-110 hejra). He is an illiterate Bedouin who was appointed as Wali of Al-Jazirah by Omar Bin Abdel-Aziz in the year 100 of hejrah. He invaded the Romans and defeated them. (Al-Tarmanini, p. 710.)

31. Abdel-Hamid Bin Yahia. He is Abdel-Hamid Al-Kateb.

32. Abu-Salamah Al-Khallal (749,132 of hejrah). He is Hafs Bin Suleiman Al-Hamadani. He lived at Darb Al-Khallalin in Kofah. He was a link between Al-Humaimah and Khrasan. When the Abbasids armies were victorious, he was appointed a prince of Khurasan. He was called "The Vizier of Aal-Muhammed." He proclaimed the Hashemite Imam. He did not pronounce the name of the caliph because he intended to deliver it to Ja'afar Al-Sadeq, and Abdullah Bin Al-Hussain, and Omar Al-Ashraf Bin Ali Zain Al-Abedeen. When Abdullah Abul-Abbas entered Al-Kofah, Abu Salamah apologized to him. Abul-Abbas accepted his apology, and planned to kill him and he did kill him afterwards. (Al-Tarmanini, p. 845.)

CHAPTER 9

Religion and Constitution in the Arab World

The Arab world lived under the Ottoman Empire for four centuries. Because the religion of the state was Islam, there was great Ottoman Cultural influence, especially in the areas of law and constitutions. Although the constitution appeared in a new era after the collapse of the Ottoman Empire, Ottoman influence was clear. England and France replaced the Ottomans in some parts of the Arab World like Syria, Lebanon, Iraq, Jordan, and Palestine in 1918, but their influence on constitutions was not as important as the Ottoman's. The first constitution in the Arab world appeared after First World War in 1918. It was the constitution of the kingdom of Syria,[1] and since then there has been an idea repeated in all the Arab constitutions, which is that the state safeguards the free exercise of all forms of worship and religious rites in accordance with the customs observed in the country, unless such exercise is inconsistent with public order or decorum. The second constitution was in Iraq, and it was the constitution of the new kingdom under Faisal the ex-king of Syria. The king and the British were interested in having a constitution since Iraq was under a British Mandate. Committees were formed for that purpose, and they concentrated on the word (law) because constitution is not an Arabic word. Article 13 mentioned that Islam is the religion of the state. The state will safeguard the freedom of others to practice their religion according to their customs unless this exercise is inconsistent with security or order in society. It guaranteed the rights of all sects to have their own schools using their own languages within the framework of the educational system of the country.[2] This was inherited from the Ottoman Constitution that appeared in 1876.[3] Until then, there had been no concentration on Arab nationalism, which appeared later in the 1950s.

Arab Nationalism and Islam

Although the 1950s witnessed a concentration on Arab nationalism, an old Ottoman expression was repeated in all the Arab states' constitutions. It stated that the freedom of religion is guaranteed on condition that it must be inconsistent with decorum or public order.[4]

Egypt

In 1930, the Egyptian constitution stated Islam is the religion of state. When a revolution took place in Egypt in 1952, the commander of the armed forces who replaced the king declared that they would safeguard freedom of religion consistent with public order, decorum, or the customs of the society. These words were repeated in the 1956 constitution. Gamal Abid El Nassir, who received Arab power in Egypt in 1953, concentrated on Arab nationalism. For the first time in Egypt, the constitution stated that Egypt was part of the Arab World.[5] For 17 years, only one constitution appeared in Egypt. In 1970, the new president, Sadat, came to power in Egypt and a new constitution appeared, repeating the same ideas about Islam and stating that Islam was the main source of legislation. It should be mentioned that the change in constitutions in Egypt related to the decisions of leaders, not to the needs of the people, because there were several changes in Egypt during the period of President Sadat.

Jordan and Morocco

Jordan has had three constitutions in 1928, 1946, and 1952. The constitution of 1952 repeated the same Ottoman idea regarding religion, which is repeated in the Moroccan constitution.

The Experience of Syria and Tunisia

Syria and Tunisia were under the control of the French before independence. Both concentrated on the religion of the president and stated that the religion of president was Islam.[6] Tunisia got its independence in 1957. In the beginning, the constitution stated that the religion of the king was Islam. A year later the text stated that the religion of the state and the religion of the president was Islam. It safeguarded practicing religion in the framework of not violating public security, decorum, or customs. Syria, who was under a French mandate, had its first constitution in 1930. It stated that the religion of the president was Islam. All the constitutions in 1930, 1950, 1953, 1962, and 1964 concentrated on the same idea. When discussions took place to separate religion from the state to comply with democracy, the result was a statement by the parliament that the religion of the president was Islam. In 1979, the Assembly of People suggested canceling the idea of the religion of the president to comply with secularism, but President Haffiz Al Asad sent a long letter saying that Islam is the religion of love, progress, equality, and social security. In the history of Syria there have been two occasions when this idea was ignored: in 1958 when Syria and Egypt were united, and in 1969.[7]

Sudan

In Sudan, Article 16 in the constitution says that Islam is the religion of the Majority and Christianity is the religion of a high number of people. The government guaranteed the freedom of all the other religions without discrimination.[8]

The Gulf States

The Gulf States had their independence in the 1960s and 70s in the era of Arab Nationalism. In spite of that, the constitutions repeated the same ideas regarding safeguarding the freedom of religion. For example, the Kuwaiti constitution stated that Islam is the religion of the state and the prince of Kuwait must be a descendent of Moslem parents.[9] There were other articles which dealt with respecting Arabic and Islamic heritage. In the United Arab Emirates, the same ideas were repeated in 1971. The constitution stated that Islam is the official religion and th freedom of religion is guaranteed on the condition it does not violate the public order, decorum, or customs of society.[10] In 1970, the Qatar constitution stated that the religion of state is Islam, which was also the source of legislation, and that the government would work to deepen the roots of Islam.[11] In Bahreen, the same ideas existed, and the government promised to protect religious places and meetings that were consist with customs.[12] Oman repeated the same ideas regarding Islam as the religion of state and the main source of legislation, and it guaranteed freedom of religion in the framework of not violating public orders or customs .

Saudi Arabia, Yemen, and Libya

Saudi Arabia repeated the same Ottoman idea regarding the religion of state is Islam and it is the main source of legislation,[13] which is repeated in the Yemen constitution; and it stated that the personal affairs of non Moslims was left to special law. In Libya, the constitution stated that the Holy Quran is the law of the society.[14]

Lebanon

Lebanon's experience in the Arab would precede others. The Ottoman Empire authorized the Lebanese to administer their own country in the fifteenth century. This situation continued until the regional and global powers entered Lebanon, and disorder appeared in 1864 when the Ottomans appointed a non-Lebanese Christian governor in Lebanon for 5 years. He was assisted by twelve Lebanese who represented all sects in Lebanon. When the first Lebanese constitution was declared in 1926 under the French mandate, traditions in Lebanon took into consideration some of the ideas adopted by the ottomans in forming government. The president of Lebanon is a Maronite Christian by traditions. The prime minister is Sunni Moslem by the same procedures.[15]

Arab Nationalism

By the end of the 1950s, the scope of Arab nationalism was very wide and new trends appeared in the Arab world. There was unity between Iraq and Jordan, and unity between Egypt and Syria in 1958. The Pan Arabism led by Egypt was very successful. There was a pro-Egypt revolt in Iraq. A new constitution was written by an officer in two weeks, which was influenced by the constitution of the new state, United Arab Republic, which was formed between Syria and Egypt. Although the new Iraqi constitution ignored religion, the debates in the cabinet concentrated on the idea that Islam is the religion of state and freedom of religion was guaranteed. Between 1963 and 1970, four constitutions appeared in Iraq. The first one, which was called the law of the revolutionary officers' council, appeared in 1963 after the coup of army officers. A year later another law replaced the previous one. It concentrated on the equality of people regardless of their religion, language, or race. A new constitution appeared in 1968 when the Baath Party received power under the leadership of the two officers. The constitution stated that Islam is the religion of state, and it guaranteed freedom of religion in the framework of not violating public order. In 1970. a new constitution appeared that reflected the Baath party philosophy. In 1990, the new constitution stated the same ideas but added new things including that freedom of religion must be inconsistent with public interest. Article 58 warned any party from isolating Iraq from its Arabic environment by mixing religion and politics.

Conclusion

We have noticed that the same ideas were repeated over the years, starting from the early 1920s, and all versions of the constitution declared freedom of religion. This reflected the idea which appeared for the first time in the Ottoman era, in 1876, to guarantee freedom of religion within a framework of not violating the morals or customs of society. This idea was repeated in most of the Arab constitutions; we have seen that the change of leaders in the Arab world was the basic reason for changing the constitutions, not the basic needs of the people.

Notes

1. The constitution of Syria in 1918. See (Dasteer, El Dowal Arabi, Cairo: The Arab League, 1955).

2. The Constitution of Iraq in 1925, articles 2, 4, 9, and 10.

3. The Ottoman Constitution 1876.

4. The Constitution of Jordan article 1.

5. Dastour El Shaab (The People's Constitution 1955, Cairo: The Information Dept.; M. Khalil, El Nozim El Sayisieh Wa El Qanoon El Daitouri, Egypt n.d.; M. Abu Zaid, El Nezam El Dastouri El Massri, Alxandria: Dar El Maarif 1984.

6. Dasteer, op. cit.; Wajech El Haffar. El Dastour Wa El Hokim, Damascus n.d.; Ameen Asbir, Tatawer El Nozim El Dastourich Fi Soryieb 1946–1973, Beruit: Dar El Nahhar, pp. 117, 123, 184, 370.; El Mozaffar Wadi, El dastour Fi Tunis, Tunsia Markaz El Bchouth Wa El diras- sat 1986, pp. 39-78.

7. Asbir, op.cit,

8. Nabeel El Sani,El Ahkam El Dastourieh fi El Belad Al Arabieh, The Texts Of the Arabic Constitutions,

9. A. Hassan Mabadi El Nizam El Dastouri Fi El Kuwait, Beruit:Dar El Vahar, 1968 articles 24, 35.

10. Sani, op.cit.

11. Ibid., article 7.

12. Article 22.

13. Ibid.

14. Ibid.

15. Adasteer op. cit. and Ebrahim Shecha, El Nezam El Dastouri El Libnani, Beruit: El Dar El Gamieh 1983, p. 308.

PART 3

CHAPTER 10

Europe and the Arabs: A Sample of Cooperation Case Study
Polish – Jordanian Relationship
(Jordanian Point of View) 1935–2012

Introduction

Economic relations between Poland and Jordan preceded political relations for years. Politically, Poland had been in the satellite of the Eastern
Block since 1945, while Jordan was under the British mandate and had a
treaty with UK from 1921 until 1957. Since then, Jordan was committed to
strong bilateral relations with the USA, which replaced the UK in assisting
Jordan financially. Until 1963, Jordan had no political relationship with the
USSR. So, for 42 years, there had been no free will for Jordan to formu-
late a foreign policy toward the Eastern Block or the USSR. Even when the
nonaligned movement appeared, the late King Hussein did not follow the
nonaligned movement. He stated on several occasions that he was aligned
with the so-called Free World. Following the speeches of the king in the
1950s and early 60s, he considered the the USSR, China, and the Com-
munists as enemies to Jordan. As a matter of fact, he considered them like
Zionists. At the same time, he considered some of the Arab states who were
pro-Eastern block, like the PLO, enemies too. On several occasions, the
King stated that the United Arab Republic (Syria and Egypt) and PLO
were enemies of Jordan. Any Jordanian who belonged to the Communist
party was sent immediately to jail. This continued until 1962, when Prime
Minister Wasfi Tall tried to legalize political parties in Jordan and released
political prisoners, including members of the Jordan Communist Party. In
the early 1960s, the King expressed that had a role in combating communism. Moreover, he expressed that his goal was to save Jordan and the Middle East from communism. The USSR, in its turn under the famous leader
NIKITA KHRUSHCHEV, who determined to enter the Middle East, centered its activities on Egypt, Iraq, and Syria. Jordan occupied a secondary
importance to the USSR. This resulted from several factors: the Hashmites
kings in Jordan since 1921 carried conservative and anticommunist views.
Diplomatic relations with the USSR were established on 20 August 1963.
Even after that, Jordan continued to prefer dealing with the Western powers
and conservative Arab states like Saudi Arabia.

In March 1965, the USSR signed a cultural and technical cooperation with Jordan. The USSR opened a cultural centre in Amman. Jordan established diplomatic relations with a number of East European States like Czechoslovakia, Hungary, Bulgaria, and Yugoslav.

The King, after the 1967 war with Israel, considered the USSR a friend. But the general trend continued in the direction of the Western Block. Any contact with other states was with the consent of England or the USSR. We will observe this in the coming analysis.

Jordan and Poland, 1935 First Contact

The background of the contact between Jordan and Poland went back to the era of the British mandate. Jordan, among other states like Iraq, Syria, Lebanon, and Palestine, were under the British or French mandate. The Gulf States were under British protection. North Africa was under French or British influence or occupation.

All the Arab states were under British or French Mandate or influence. No one dared contact the Eastern Block countries. An eyewitness told me that in the UN, no Arab official could stand next to a USSR diplomat, even if he was in restaurant waiting to eat.

For the above reasons, Jordan's relations with Poland were good during the mandate until 1939, when Poland was occupied by the USSR and Germany. That period was better than the period when Jordan got independence and Poland became part of the Eastern Block. This period covers the years 1939 until 1964. In this period, Jordan and Poland were moving in different directions in foreign policy until the mid-1960s

But during the mandate Jordan had no constraints to contact Poland as long as Poland was on good terms with the West. I found early contact and a relationship between the two states during the mandate. This contact started while Jordan's hands were tied with the mandate under the British umbrella.

Recent Contact According to their Official Documents

When I went to the Foreign Office on the 5th of April 2012 to review the files of the Jordan – Poland bilateral relationship, I found three fat files concentrating on the recent bilateral relationship. There are three studies in the files about the very recent bilateral relationship. These short studies were written by three different persons on several occasions between the early nineties and 2004. The first was written by the director of the European department and sent to the House of Senate before the visit of the Polish delegation to the Jordanian Senate.The second and the third were written by the Jordanian charge'd affairs in Poland. All the studies were very short and similar to short reports. They give an idea about the concentrations of cooperation. But they did not cover the history before the establishment of the relationship in 1964.

The Documents of the National Library

The documents of the National Library in Amman and the official newspaper covered the history of the old relationship before 1964. The first treaty or agreement between Poland and Jordan was in 1935. Jordan was under the British mandate. There was a commercial agreement between England and Poland signed on 24 July 1935. The Jordan prince Abdulla the Founder (Later King) issued a decree that Jordan was included in this agreement.

The First Consulate

The first piece of news about the first consulate in Jordan was declared on the first of July 1937, when the official newspaper mentioned on the same day that Poland appointed a general Consul in Amman. The name of this General Consul was Witold Hollanki. He was appointed with another two General Consuls. They were the Turkish and Hungarian consuls. I didn't find any other resource that gives information about this subject. The Foreign Ministry files don't mention a word about the subject. I may assume that Poland, who needed the phosphate, started this relationship three years before establishing phosphate mining in Jordan.

The Third Activity

The third activity between Poland and Jordan was when Nazi Germany invaded Poland from the starting World War II on the 1st of September 1939, and two weeks later the USSR invaded Poland from the east. Poland fought for a month against these two powers. The declaration of Jordan on the second of December1939 stated that Polish lands were occupied by an enemy. The official paper number 656 dated 2nd DEC 1939 published this, which was never mentioned elsewhere according to my research so far.

These three activities came in the second part of the 1930s, at a time when Jordan had a strong relationship with England. Jordan was under the British mandate by then. Nothing could have happened without the consent of the British government. It is true that Jordan was under mandate, and did not have full sovereignty, but the prince (the King of Jordan, who is called the Founder, was with the free world and the Jordan Arab Legion fought with the free world in Iraq and Syria). Jordan was the sole country in the area that was not protected by any foreign power, and which was stable during the World War II. This accelerated Jordanian demands to request that England grant Jordan independence, which it got in 1946.

The Moslems in Poland in 1942

In the National Library there is a letter sent from Istanbul on 26 March 1942. This letter was forwarded to the Head of the Prince Court. The letter concentrated on the Germans' harsh treatment towards the Moslems in Poland, who had lived 500 years peacefully with their Polish brothers before the Germans came and started these procedures towards the Moslems. They closed their mosques and used these mosques as carnage for their war. They prevented Moslems from praying the 5 daily prays. According to the letter, the Moslem Mufti in Poland protested against this, but he was humiliated by the Germans after doing so. The delegation that was sent to the German Authority in Poland was killed by them before listening to the complaint.

Diplomatic Relations

Diplomatic relations were established between Jordan and Poland in 1964. According to the archive of the National Library in Jordan, the diplomatic relationship started on 25th March 1964. This piece of news was mentioned in the official newspaper on the same date. According to a personal conservation with the ex-Polish diplomat Jan Natkanski, he said that Poland by then had sent him from Baghdad (Iraq). He had just finished his BA and graduated from Baghdad University when he left Baghdad to participate in a commercial office in Amman.

The first Polish ambassador presented his credentials to his majesty the late king Hussein in January 1965. The Polish ambassadors to Jordan were accredited from Beirut; later they were accredited from Damascus. The first ambassador presented his paper to His Majesty Abdullah the second in December of 2003. Before that the Polish embassy was headed by charge d'affairs.

The Early Cooperation in Phosphate in 1961

The Phosphate Factor Again

In the National Library documents, there are some indicators about early cooperation between Jordan and Poland in 1961. I found a document referring to the phosphate factor in the relationship between Poland and Jordan. The Chairman of the Board of the Phosphate Company sent a letter on 7 December 1961 requesting the Prime Minister accelerate granting the visas to the Polish clients who came to Jordan from the commercial section in Beirut, Lebanon, or elsewhere. He complains that the Ministry of Interior did not issue visas quickly. He requested that he issue visas for the clients of the three states: Poland, Yugoslavia, and Czechoslovakia. He wrote to the prime minister that these three states were the most important market for Jordan. They imported more than half of the Jordanian phosphate exports. That increased year after year.[2]

Regarding the Phosphate History

Jordan is a very rich in its phosphate deposits. The first discovery was in 1894. Jordan produced phosphate in 1934 at the Rusaifah mines, located between Amman and Zarqa. Up to the mid-1980s, phosphate was produced at three sites in Jordan. The reserves inflated day after day. In 1968, production rose to 1.16 million tons, which was five times more than production in 1956. Production increased to 1.76 million tons. In 1985, production rose to 5.92 million tons. In 1986 and 1987 production rose to 6.25 and 6.7 million tons. The production never reached this level when it collapsed later as following:

1988 -------6.5 million tons

1990--------6.2 million tons

1991--------5.0 million tons

1992--------5.2 million tons

1993--------4.3 million tons

1994--------4.2 million tons

1995--------5.0 million tons

1996-------5.4 million tons

1997--------5.8 million tons

1998--------5.9 million tons

Phosphate exports retreated in Jordan because Poland couldn't import phosphate after the collapse of the Eastern Block. We may observe the high percentage of phosphate exports from Jordan to Poland between 1984 and 1998 when Poland was the highest among the Eastern Block states.

Direction of Jordanian Phosphate exports (Thousand tons)

	Bulgaria	Poland	Czechoslovakia	Romania	Yugoslavia	(Russia)
1984	69	225	112	861	342	
1985	93	333	116	684	233	
1986	46	424	119	590	571	
1987	-	899	73	503	543	
1989	46	555	116	539	707	
1990	-	-	94	130	287	71
1991	30	135	12	61	186	242
1992	61	140	-	82	236	71
1993	58	-	-	-	93	-
1994	67	-	-	13	52	-
1995	69	-	-	70	-	-
1996	139	59	-	13	52	-
1997	218	-	-	70	-	-
1998	97	-	-	-	23	-

The source is Muhammad Azhar, "Phosphate Exports by Jordan," *Arab Studies Quarterly*, Vol. 22, Number 4 (Fall 2000): p. 59.

Poland was the highest importers in the years 1987 and 1989. Then the imports collapsed. When Poland did not import Jordanian phosphate during the years 1994–1997, the growth in Jordanian phosphate exports became slower than growth in world phosphate exports. When Poland imported high amounts of phosphate from Jordan during the years 1986 and 1989, the growth of the Jordanian exports was higher than the growth of the world exports.

Phosphate is the most important export in the Jordanian export basket. Potash is another mineral product that was the second most important commodity on the Jordanian list of exports. The absence of Poland affected all the issues of the exporting of phosphate.

The direction of the phosphate exports from Jordan was affected as follows:

In 1984---------East Europe imported 28% of Jordan's Phosphate

In 1998--------East Europe imported 2.0% of Jordan's Phosphate

Poland imports almost stopped in 1991 after it was the highest among 20 Western and Eastern European states in the years 1987 and 1989.

Poland was not able to find the hard currency to pay Jordan to buy phosphate or potash. According to the Jordanian resources in the official files, the Jordanians refused the idea of exchanging goods.

So, the early cooperation gave great concentration on economic cooperation and great importance was attached to the economic cooperation.[3]

The Second Station in Cooperation 1967

In the documents of the national library, a document revealed a significant kind of contact of the political and small issues. You may find Poland granted the phosphate company a car and other issues. For example:

In 1967, the Minister of Telecommunication addressed the foreign minister in his letter dated 2 Nov 1967. He is referring to the letter issued by the ITU (International Telecommunication Union) on 16 October 1967, which says that Poland and Pakistan will not accept any letter which had stamps that glorified Israeli aggression on Arab states. Poland informed the ITU that she would write on these letters not accepted and return them. The Jordan Ministry of Telecommunication suggested that the Arab Telecommunication Union should evaluate the actions of Poland and Pakistan and send thanks to them for their position, which stated that Poland and Pakistan would not receive these letters and send them back.4

The Era of King Hussein

King Hussein ascended to the throne in 1952. It was a coincidence that a small Jordanian phosphate company was recognized by the government in the same year. It became Jordan Phosphate Mines Company at Al Rusayfah. Between 1953 and 1956, the production increased sharply and doubled.[5]

By then, Poland was importing phosphate although the relationship with the Eastern block was not working. King Hussein couldn't establish a political relation with the USSR in the '50s because that may conflict with US assistance to Jordan. The USSR in return was attacking Jordan policy as "pro west," "reactionary" and "substantive to imperialism."[6] In spite of that, the era of King Hussein was the golden era of phosphate exchange with Poland. This was not affected by the cold war between the two blocks. Just the reverse—when the cold war was over, Polish imports collapsed in unexpected way. Anyway, Jordan and Poland concentrated on the economic issues regardless of the diplomatic relations, which has not started until late. Jordan had not opened a resident embassy in Poland although they started talks in 1962. In 1962, Jordan and Poland started talk to have a bilateral relationship.[7] On 25 May 1964, diplomatic relations started (the Jordanian official paper mentioned this date).

Economy and Communication Affairs

A review of official visits or agreements revealed a concentration on economic and commercial affairs. In a report in 1977, it is revealed that the relationship concentrated on commercial affairs. There was a commercial agreement between Jordan and Poland in 1977. The royal decree agreed on 6 Dec 1978 regarding transportations (the writer has photocopy of this agreement). Between (1993–1995) there was no hard currency for Poland, and the imports retreated. According to Jordanian official documents, an Austrian company in 1992 assisted importing phosphate. The attempt to exchange sulfur for phosphate with Jordan failed because the sulpher price was high. The international trans ammonia in 1997 bought 125.00 tons of phosphate to be sold by the Polish company.[8]

According to the official report in general, there were several agreements. Most of them were in the 1990s.Tthe official report listed the following:

1. In February 1964, a cultural relationship established. Nothing about the details of this in the Jordanian documents.

2. In 1977 there was an agreement (mentioned above).

3. Agreement on air transport signed in 1993 and entered into force in 2006. The Royal decree was issued on 18 Jan 1994 (the writer has photocopy of this agreement).

4. Agreement on avoidance of the double taxation signed in 1997 and entered in force in 1999. The Royal decree approved this on 21st Oct 1997 (the writer has a copy of this agreement).

5. Agreement on mutual support and protection of the investments signed in 1997. The Royal decree approved this on 18 November 1997 (the writer has a copy of this agreement).

6. Agreements on cooperation in tourism (signed in June 2004,

and entered into force in 2006)[9] (the writer has a copy of this agreement).

The Royal decree approved this on 16 May 2005.

Development after 2003

In April 2003, Poland signed an agreement and became a member state of the European union on May 1, 2004. Poland started the transformation of its political and economic system from the authoritarian rule of the communist party and planned economy to the parliamentary multiparty system and free market.[10] Poland drove close cooperation with Europe and at the same time, Jordan was getting closer to Europe and joined Barcelona's process developing associated cooperation between the European union and the Mediterranean countries of North Africa and the Middle East. In November 1997, Jordan and Europe concluded an agreement which entered into force in May 2002.[11]

Jordan was one of the beneficiaries of the programs MEDA I and MEDA II to assist the Mediterranean countries. In 2007, the EU introduced its European neighborhood policy in the Mediterranean states. Jordan, who is among these states, started to negotiate the national action plans which concluded for the years 2007–2010 and which stipulate the allocation of 295 million euros as assistance to Jordan during this period. The successful implementation of the action plan permitted Jordan to obtain advanced status in relations with the EU and starts a new action plan for the years 2010–2015.[12] This advanced status provided a new dimension to the bilateral relations between both friendly states.[13] In the framework of EU assistance to other states, Poland helped Jordan to construct and equipd libraries within the framework of the Jordanian program (*maktabli*) in 2009, 2010 (and 2011).[14]

The Triangle Jordan–Poland–EU

Writers and politicians talk about the Jordan–Poland–EU triangle; they say that Poland's relationship is closer to the EU and since 2004 it is within this dominant framework.[15]

Natkanski says that not all in this triangle are equal; he was referring to the bilateral relations between the two sides. Poland took the initiative to make Poles and Jordanians know each other.

Since 2009, when assistant professor Krezyszt of Bojko, the charge d' affaires of the republic of Poland chaired his mission, he had a several initiatives that contributed to helping Jordanians and Poles know each other. Direct contrasts and cooperation between universities were started in these frames:

Conferences

By the initiative of the Polish Embassy in Jordan, several conferences took places:

1. The first Poland–Jordan–European Union: Future Aspects (December 10, 2010) organized by the University of Jordan in Amman–Jordan and the Jagiellonian University in Krakow and the embassy of Poland in Amman.[16]

2. The second conference: Aspects of Cooperation and Mutual Experience of Relations, the Second International Conference on December 15, 2011, organized by the University of Jordan and the Embassy of the Republic of Poland.[17]

The purpose of these conferences is to share with friends from Jordan, including Jordanian academics, experiences with Polish achievements. The conference is an excellent venue to exchange views on the current situation in the region and provide opportunities to deepen bilateral relations between Polish universities and representatives from the worlds of science.[18]

The private sector participated to deepen the cooperation. (JEBA) Jordan Europe business association organized ten Polish-Jordanian Business Forums in Jordan during the period (2000–2010) and a trade mission to Poland during May 2011. This reflected joint efforts between the Polish and Jordanian private sectors, which resulted from the close cooperation of JEBA and the Polish Embassy in Amman.[19]

Cultural Cooperation

There are several names in the field of cultural cooperation from both sides. There are Polish and Jordan names which witnessed several fields of cooperation in economics, cultural affairs, education, business, and tourism. In cultural affairs, there are several names on each side; from the Polish side there is the late Antoni Ostrasz (1923–1996), who devoted many years of his life to Jerash.[20]

In Poland, it is still remembered that the first ever student from an Arab country in Poland after World War II was a Jordanian citizen who became Professor Saleh Hamarneh.[21]

The Reports and Notes about the Jordan-Poland Relationship in the Foreign Office

There are several studies and reports about Jordan and Poland:

1. The first note is from Sami Lash in 1992; he pointed out that Poland faced problems finding hard currency to import phosphate. In his report, he conveyed the Polish point of view when he said that the foreign policy of any state toward any other state doesn't mean that it is convinced with this policy of this state. He is referring to the Poland-Israel relationship.

Jordan and Poland relationship:

In the file of Jordan and Poland's relationship, there is a great interest and continuity of following up the relationship.[22]

2. The second report was written by charge d'affaires; he referred to the meeting of the speaker of the Upper House with the Minster of Foreign Affairs in July 1999, who expressed his wishes to increase the parliamentary visits between the two states.

On April 2000, there is a note about 4 students who want to study Arabic.[23]

According to the charge d'affairs, the relation between Jordan and Poland is very limited.[24]

3. There is another report by Yosef Batayneh from 2004. He pointed out the following ideas:
   - Cultural relationship started in February 1964.
   - He mentioned the agreements in 1977, 1993, 1997, and 2004.
   - He pointed out that there are no problems in relationship.[25]

The Ambassadors of Jordan and Poland
The First Jordanian Ambassador

The first ambassador was appointed in August 1971; he was nonresident ambassador assigned in Moscow. In 2004, the ambassador to Warsaw had been transferred from Moscow to Berlin. The speaker of the upper house in Warsaw, Alicja Crezeskowlok, thanked the Jordanian ambassador, Saleh Irshaydat, in the meeting with him on 16 November 2000 for that. Berlin is closer to Warsaw than Moscow.[26]

The Fourth Report by the Head of the European Department

This report was written by the head of the European Department, Mr. Nabeel Talhouni, on 7th November 2000; the note referred to the history of diplomatic relations between Jordan and Poland. The Polish ambassador in Damascus was the nonresident Polish ambassador in Jordan. Jordan's ambassador in Moscow by then is the nonresident ambassador to Warsaw. He pointed out that Poland was interested in buying potash through exchange of Polish goods, but this was not accepted by the Jordanian potash company.[27]

Several Issues

Between Jordan and Poland, several issues were mentioned in correspondence, such as:

1. Economic issues like requesting information to establish a stock Polish Company in Jordan.

2. Inviting Jordanian ministries to attend conferences in Poland on combating terrorism; it is mentioned that ambassador Omayah Toqan in (Vienna) to attend this conference which ended with Warsaw Declaration November 6th 2001.

The Activities in 2004

This year 2004 was the anniversary of 40 years since establishing diplomatic relation between Poland and Jordan; it witnessed several activities which reached six important activities between the two states. King Abdullah 11 visited Poland on 1st September 2004. The King had a meeting with the Polish president in which they discuss economic, military, and cultural cooperation. The King welcomed the idea of the Polish president having a joint businessmen council. In the meeting with the prime minister, the King welcomed touristic, economic, and cultural cooperation. He welcomed paving the way for the Polish businessmen who wanted to invest in Jordan or Iraq. In this visit, Dr. Marwan El Moasher, the Foreign

Affairs Minister, met his counterpart and discussed opening a consulate for Jordan in Warsaw with him.[28]

The Meeting between Jordanian Officials and Polish Businessmen

The King attended a meeting between Jordanian officials and Polish businessmen and mentioned the following ideas:

1. Jordan achieved 7.2 % of growth in the first half of 2004.
2. The opportunities to invest in Jordan or Iraq was mentioned again by the King.
3. The King referred to the investment in education, where the cost was half a billion dollars. The King said Jordan developed software in electronic education and sold it to New Jersey.
4. The King said that Jordan is committed to partnership with Iraq in trade; Al Aqaba port is importing what Iraq needs; there is a plan to build the first highway and free zone area on the border with Iraq.
5. The King said that Jordan assists Eyad Allawi, who presided over the Iraqi government then; this government classified her agenda with her priorities. Jordan supported Eyad Allawi's government to achieve stability in Iraq

The Jordanian government and Poland signed an executive program for cooperation in the cultural science and education fields for the years 2004–2006; originally this agreement was signed in 1977.

The King attended a formal dinner invitation from the Polish president, who welcomed the King saying, "This is the first visit by a Jordanian monarch." He added that this visit came after 40 years of an official relationship between the two states. The King stated that he was committed to rebuild a unified, democratic Iraq and to participate in combating terrorism. The King invited the Polish president to Jordan.[29]

The Ambassadors

Jordan has not established an embassy yet. The embassy in Berlin has been covering activities in Poland since 2004. Before this, the job was assigned to the embassy in Moscow as follows:

1. The Ambassador – Kamal al Homoud

27 February 1975

2. The Ambassador – Hani Khasawneh
3 February 1978

3. The Ambassador – Faleh El Taweel
18 April 1984

4. The Ambassador – Mohammad Affash Al Adwan
18 April 1991

5. The Ambassador – Khaldoun Al-Dhair
7 September 1994

From Berlin

1. Charge d' affaires – Qassem Okour
13 December1998

2. The Ambassador – Saleh Rusheidat
18 March 2004

3. Charge d'affaires – Yousef Bateineh
1 August 2005

4. The Ambassador – Isaa Nasser Ayyoub
31 July 2009

The Polish Ambassadors or charge d'affairs in Jordan

1. The Ambassdor – Witold Skuratowicz
11 January 1965

2. Franciszek Onichowski
11 January 1965

3. The Ambassador – Zdzisia Wojcik
9 May 1966

4. Pawel Stafer
1 January 1970

5. Edward Czapula
1 December 1971

6. The Ambassador – Tadeusz Wujek
28 March1973

7. Tadeusz Krzeminski
1 May 1974

8. The Ambassador – Antoni Pierzchala
   21 June1975

9. The Ambassador – Stanislaw Matosek
   29 June 1977

10. The Ambassador – Boguslaw Kaczyinski
    15 November 1982

11. Jacck Szydlowski
    1 August 1984

12. Marian Dabrowski
    31 October 1986

13. The Ambassador –LudWik Janczyszyn
    18 March 1987

14. Marian Dabrowski
    19 July 1987

15. The Ambassador – Jozef Baryla
    7 June 1989

16. Edmund Pawalk
    19 July 1990

17. The Ambassador – Krzystof Balinski
    16 October 1991

18. Boguslaw Rekas
    12 September 1995

19. The Ambassador – Stainslaw Pawlak
    20 February 1997

20. Mariusz Wozniak
    5 July 1999

21. Magdalena Renata Pienkos
    21 September 2003

22. The Ambassador – Andrzej Biera
    9 December 2003

23. Krzystof Bojoko
    7 May 2009

The source of the names of the Ambassadors in both states is The Ministry of Foreign Affairs in Poland. The documents are represented by his Excellency Associate. Prof Krzystof Bojoko. PS wherever the rank is not mentioned above, the rank is charge d'affaires.

Conclusions and Remarks

Jordan and Poland started their relationship in the mid-1930s. This relationship did not develop in a strong bilateral relationship. The two states are too far apart geographically. Until now, there has been no direct airline route from Amman to Warsaw or vice versa. In different times, there were constraints on a free bilateral relationship between the two states Jordan and Poland; for example, at an early stage between 1935 and 1939, it echoed the British relationship with England. Later after War World II, Poland was a USSR satellite state, while Jordan was in the Western Satellite, and the relationship was affected by these constraints until 1963 when Jordan established a relationship with the USSR.

Since then, the Polish approach or initiative toward Jordan was stronger than the Jordanian initiatives towards Poland. Until 2004, there had been no visits between the two states on the level of King or the President of Poland. Jordan sent a non-resident Ambassador from Moscow in 1975, then from Berlin in 2004. Poland sent a non-resident ambassador ten years earlier, in 1964, from Beruit and Damascus. Now Poland has a resident ambassador in Jordan; there is an embassy in Amman.

The commercial relationship in phosphate exports was strong. Poland imports of phosphate were high until the collapse of the USSR. Since then, Poland hasn't been able to find the hard currency and imports retreated. This retreat affected the percentage of the Jordanian share in the international size of exports.

The most important thing these days when the charge d'affaires of the republic of Poland, Ass. Prof Krzystof Bojoko, arrived in Jordan and staged two international conferences in Amman in one year. Jordanians scholars, journalists, and businessmen visited Poland for conferences or cultural activities. Personally, I was invited to two conferences in Poland in April and November of 2011. A Jordanian delegation visited Poland in 2010 for similar purposes. There are uncounted official visits from Poland to Jordan and vice versa. I assume this subject will be discussed by Ass. Prof Krzystof

Bojoko. The last idea comes from suggestions from Mr. Yousf Batanieh, our charge d'affaires in Poland 5 years ago, who concentrated on the idea that opening the embassy in Warsaw was very important idea—but Jordan has financial problems. He couldn't open an embassy in Sweden and other states like Denmark, which closed her embassy in Jordan.

Jordan cannot close the embassy after opening it .The embassy in Berlin covers several states like Sweden, Norway, Poland, and Denmark. The Polish side kept following up with Jordan to have embassy there. In 2004, this was discussed with the King when his Majesty visited Poland. Going back to the Europe–Jordan– UE triangle, this may ease the relationship with Poland as long as there is no embassy in Poland.

Notes

1. Ghalib, Saleh Abu Jabir. *The collection of Jordan treaties and agreements 1923–1973.* Amman: the Ministry of Culture, p. 223.

2. The head of the phosphate mines memoranda to the Prime Minister of Jordan no.8/5/1708 dated 7 November 1961.

3. Jan, Natkanski. Polish–Jordanian Relations: Glimpse from the past and the perspectives in Poland–Jordan European Union: Future Aspects Conference December 10, 2010. It appeared in the book by the same title edited by Professor Saad Abu Dayeh, and Ass. Prof. *Krzystof Bojoko*, charge d'affaires of the Republic of Poland to Jordan 2011.

4. The official memoranda by the Ministry of Communication to the Forging Ministry no. ch4\9\19625 dated 22 January 1967.

5. George, Harris. *Jordan, its people, its society, its culture.* (New Haven: Hraf Press, 1958), p. 161 .

6. Ibid., p. 161.

7. Asst. Prof. Kryzstof, charge d'affaires of the Republic of Poland to Jordan. Lecture on 1st April 2012 at el Hussein University in Maan.

8. Summary Report about the Economic and Commercial report kept in the Polish and Jordan file in the Foreign Office. It referred to an agreement dated 3 October 1977.

9. Report no. 5/3/1070 12 August 2004 written by charge d' affairs Mr. Yousef Batiuien. He referred to the development of imports and exports between Jordan and Poland as following:

	Imports	Exports
1999	4.101.392	43.857
2000	2.723.882	885.482
2001	2.545.746	1.961.175
2002	3.290.143	4.442.910
2003	4.412.539	6.901.401

10. Natkanski, op.cit p. 152.

11. Ibid.

12. Ibid.

13. Ibid., p. 152.

14. Ibid., p. 153.

15. The head of the European Department in Foreign Affairs, Mr. Husam El Husseini on 5 April 2012.

16. The works of their conference produced in a book in 2011 in the same title.

17. The works of their conference were edited in a book by Professor Saad Abu Dayeh and Ass. Prof. Krzysztof Bojoko, the head of mission of the Republic of Poland to Jordan 2012.

18. Speech by Ass Prof. Krzysztof Bojoko at the conference opening in 2011.

19. JEBA president speech at the opening of the conference 15 December 2011.

20. Bojoko, speech at the conference 10 December 2010.

21. Natkanski, op.cit.

22. Letter by Mr. Qasim el oquar, charge d'affaires 5/13/931, dated 21/4/1999.

23. Note from the embassy dated 18 April 2000.

24. Qaim, op.cit.

25. Note to Foreign Office from the Embassy in Berlin in Nov. 2000.

26. Note written by the head of the European Department in Foreign office to the General Secretary of the Senate dated 7 Novmeber 2000.

27. Jordanian Documents no 66 date 2004 (Ministry of Information), pp. 136-138.

28. Ibid., p.140.

29. Ibid., p.110.

CHAPTER 11

The Middle East Peace Process 1948–1994: Constraints and Prospects

Introduction

The aim is to explore the constraints and prospects of the Arab-Israeli peace process. It considers the developments since the establishment of Israel in 1948, when the British mandate ended, and the UN General Assembly through its Resolution No. 181, divided Palestine and created the state of Israel. The Arabs rejected the resolution and started their struggle for a Palestinian state. Since then, they have fought six wars with Israel.

The first war, fought on 15 May 1948, went in favour of Israel, and the Arab states had to sign the Armistice Agreement. After the war the United Nations tried to reach a permanent peace by converting the just concluded Armistice Agreement into a permanent peace settlement. But the United Nations failed in its efforts. The Arabs did not comprehend the idea of an Israeli state and felt that it was a conspiracy by the colonial powers to occupy their lands by force.

In 1956, Egypt faced a triple aggression from Israel, England, and France. Israel occupied Sinai but was forced by political pressure especially from the US to withdraw.

In 1967, Egypt, Syria, Iraq, and Jordan entered the third war against Israel, who defeated the four armies and occupied the Sinai peninsula, the Golan Heights, West Bank, and the Gaza Strip. This war changed the strategy and goals of the Arabs. They asked Israel to withdraw from the territories it had occupied in 1967. They did not demand the territories occupied in 1948. On 22 November 1967, Security Council Resolution 242 proposed an ambiguous formula for the peace negotiations. The English text of the resolution mentioned "Territories" instead of "the territories which were occupied by Israel in the 1967 war." As a result, the conflict of how to interpret the word territories emerged, with each side adopting a different point of view. In 1968, Israeli Premier Yigal Allon approached the so-called moderate Arabs and asked them to accept a peace plan which called for absorption of some 40 percent of the West Bank to buttress Israel's security. His plan was rejected. Egypt waged the Attrition War against Israel during the years 1967–1970. This war led the way for the Nixon administration, which had come to power in 1969, to search for a sustainable peace. In August 1970, American Secretary of State William Roger put forth his famous peace initiative, which was rejected by both Egypt and Syria.

In October 1973, Egypt and Syria waged a fourth war against Israel. Jordan also indirectly took part in this war, which created a much different political climate for settlement of the historic Arab-Israeli conflict. Security Council Resolution 242 was reaffirmed by the new Resolution 338.

The Arabs felt redeemed and recovered the self-confidence they had lost in 1967. Israel realized the heavy cost of the wars with Arabs and agreed to strive for a peaceful settlement of the Middle East crisis. The climate became more conducive for peace.

Geneva Conference

The prominent result of the 1973 war was that it paved the way for the Geneva Conference. The diplomatic efforts of the Nixon administration resulted in a peace conference which was held in Geneva in December 1973, under the auspices of the UN, and was co-chaired by the US and USSR.[1] Among the Arab states, Jordan, Egypt, and Lebanon participated in the plenary session. Syria declined to participate. The aim of the conference was to establish a just and durable peace in the Middle East. However, the conference was adjourned after the initial round of speech making before any discussion on the issue of Palestinian representation could take place. Palestinians had expected recognition of their right to self-determination, but since they were represented by other participants, no progress was made over the issue.

Step by Step Diplomacy

The US diplomats conducted bilateral negotiations to disengage the military forces along the October cease-fire line. Within two years, the following three agreements were reached by the three parties that is Syria, Egypt, and Israel.

1. In January 1974, the Egyptian-Israeli Agreement was signed.

2. In May 1974, the Syrian-Israeli Agreement was signed.

3. In 1975, the Sinai Interim Agreement was signed.

In 1976, however, the step by step diplomacy came to a halt as President Nixon was forced out of office and the Geneva Conference could not be reconvened.

President Carter's Priorities

When President Carter came to power in 1976, he made the reconvening of the Geneva Conference one of his priorities.[2] During the first nine months of his tenure in office, he concentrated much of his energy on this goal and on resolving the difficult issue of Palestinian representation.

Peace Treaty between Israel and Egypt

A treaty of peace between Israel and Egypt was signed on 26 March 1979. The two states recognized each other as legitimate adversaries. Although the treaty was viewed a success as far as the American diplomacy was concerned, conflicts remained in the Middle East. The Arab countries boycotted Egypt and the climate for a lasting peace did not improve. During the same period, the Arabs and Israelis entered the bloodiest war in the Middle East history,[3] and Syria was entangled in Lebanon, so three of the principal Arab countries facing Israel remained occupied with other priorities and Arab attention was diverted towards Iran. All these factors weakened the Arab pressure on Israel. In the early eighties, Arab priorities centered on Iran-Iraq war Egypt was readmitted in the Arab world after Iraq asked for Egyptian military assistance. Syria and Libya took the side of Iran in this war, and the Arab world became divided. Israel capitalized upon this lack of solidarity among the Arabs. It attacked Lebanon in June 1982 and forced Lebanon to sign a peace treaty which did not last. In the midst of this chaos, the United States proposed its third peace initiative in September 1982. The objective of the initiative was to achieve peace in Lebanon and the West Bank, Gaza Strip, and Golan Heights. President Reagan supported this initiative by means of American military intervention in Lebanon. However, this action proved to be imprudent[4] and all-American efforts failed for a while. Once again the state of "no peace and no war" reappeared.

The US downgraded the importance of the conflict,[5] and Arabs were not able to put pressure on the US to reconvene the peace conference until 1985, when some changes including the reconciliation between Jordan and Egypt, the agreement between Jordan and the PLO to coordinate the peace effort, and the reconciliation between the PLO and the Egypt took place.

In 1984, President Reagan was re-elected. Since it had been his second term in office as President, he was free from domestic pressure and could do as he wished in the Middle East.[6] Thus, climate appeared more conducive for American political intervention. The Reagan Administration showed much interest in the occupied territories like the West Bank and Gaza Strip. Secretary of State, George Shultz was concerned with improving life in the West Bank. He pressured the Israelis to reopen the Arab owned Cairo-Amman Bank in order to provide seed money for industrial entrepreneurs.[7] However, the US concentrated on the Palestinians who were living inside the occupied territories, while ignoring the outsiders, thus denying the PLO the recognition, as the representative of Palestinians.

Insiders and Outsiders

Since 1985, the American foreign policy regarding peace in the occupied territories of the West Bank and Gaza Strip, concentrated on the insiders who had been under Israeli occupation and who lived under conditions different from the outsiders. During the years 1967–1983 there were 173,000 insiders who fled to the Gulf states, and between 1983–1985 there were 23,000 who fled to Europe and South America. Those who left were mostly women and older people. Thus, the male-female ratio in the West Bank and Gaza Strip changed dramatically. Of those who remained, 70 percent were Palestinians under the age of 24.[8] The young men were the need of a new phenomena in the West Bank and Gaza Strip. This phenomena, which emerged during late 1987, came to be known as Intifada, was directed against the Israeli soldiers. Although it was viewed by some as an ineffective means to face Israel, the Intifada gained the reputation of a heroic movement aimed at forcing Israel to recognize the Palestinian rights.

Effect of Intifada on the Peace Process

The Intifada (shake off) protest against the Israeli soldiers proved an ineffective means of resistance. The weak Arabs, however, accepted Intifada and considered it as the most heroic movement in recent Arab history.

However, the Intifada was not of any advantage to the Palestinian cause. In fact it proved advantageous for US diplomacy, which concentrated on the insiders (Palestinians in occupied territories). Although the US had started negotiating with the PLO with the assistance of the Jordanian government, the talks failed when the PLO refused to accept Resolution 242 and when the US refused to clearly define the Palestinian right of self-determination. The dialogue failed in 1986. It was shortly after the Intifada movement that the US and Israel started exploring other options for developing policies in the West Bank and the Gaza Strip. The insiders revived the Palestinian movement.[9] In this way, the Intifada influenced the foreign policy of the PLO which previously was unwilling to enter any direct dialogue with the US and adopt a moderate point of view.

Other factors which helped the US to concentrate on the peace process, included:

The end of Iran-Iraq War on 20 July 1988. The outbreak of war had attracted American attention and led to US intervention in the Gulf. The US military reflagged the Kuwaiti ships to protect them from Iran.[10] Other major events also worried Israel including the development of poison gas by Iraq and Syria's arms programs. With the end of the war, worries about the arms race were lessened.

King Hussein declared Jordan's disengagement from the West Bank on 30 July 1988; this was a great change in Jordan's foreign policy since the West Bank had been incorporated with Jordan since 1956.

In November 1988 the Palestine National Council announced in Algeria the creation of an independent Palestinian state and Yasser Arafat was designated Chairman of the State. This led Arafat to abandon the armed struggle which the PLO had declared against Israel since 1964 when the organization came into being. Moreover, he accepted the idea of coexistence with Israel. In December 1988, he reaffirmed this. In a clear way, these events encouraged the new administration in the US to approach Middle East peace from a new angle. The US took the dramatic decision to open dialogue with the PLO. It was the toughness of the US that forced the PLO to adopt a more moderate position. In May 1989, the Arab Summit Conference endorsed the Palestinian's acceptance of the proposed two-states solution. For the first time in the history of the Arab-Israel conflict, the struggle was not over the same piece of territory. Since the internal landscape of Israel did not support negotiations with the Palestinians until 1989, the US looked for another way to help create conditions for peace between Israel and Arabs and in this connection sought the help of the Soviets.[11]

The Effect of the Gulf Crisis on the Peace Process

The Gulf crisis had a direct effect on the peace process and played a major role in achieving peace in the region. After Iraqi army entered Kuwait on 2 August 1990 and declared Kuwait to be a part of Iraq.[12] The Iraqi President, Saddam Hussein, offered a linkage between his withdrawal from Kuwait and Israeli withdrawal from occupied territories. Although the US President, George Bush, rejected the linkage, he announced a Middle East peace initiative in his address to the Congress in March 1991.[13]

The Role of the Two Superpowers

During the Gulf crisis, the two superpowers played an important role by co-sponsoring the Madrid Peace Conference on Middle East, which was called on 30 October 1991. The discussions between the two superpowers over the Arab-Israel issue had started early as 1986; however, the decision to work together for a Middle East settlement came during the Gulf crisis, in September 1990. In March 1991, the two superpowers began making plans for the Madrid Conference and they also prepared the draft of the peace settlement for the Conference, which was very similar to the final version.[13] The significant thing about the peace process was that it did not carry any vestiges of a Soviet-US confrontation.[14] The situation after the Gulf crisis helped the US be in a commanding position. The US mobilized all its diplomatic efforts to create the opportunity for peace.[15] It was not the maturity of the parties concerned that brought them to Madrid, but the great skill of the American administration in dealing with the post-Gulf War crisis. The American Secretary of State, James Baker, addressed Congress in the spring of 1991, reflecting on America's firm stand of not accepting any excuse from any party. The Arab parties were prepared to come to Madrid and Israelis recognized that they had no choice.[16]

Bilateral and Multilateral Talks

The best distinction between the two kinds of talks which started in Madrid was put forth by the Israeli Foreign Minister, Shimon Peres, who said, "While the bilateral talks concerned problems of the past, multilateral talks have to do with problems of the region's future that could be solved by joint efforts." [17]

The Middle East peace process after the Madrid Conference revolved around bilateral talks between Israel and other Arab parties such as the Syrians, Lebanese, Palestinians, and the Jordanians. Syria and Lebanon wanted to recover territory that Israel had occupied in 1967, while the Palestinians focused on the creation of an independent Palestinian state, and Jordan tried to normalize its sensitive relationship with the Palestinians and Israelis alike.[18] The prime interest of Israel was security and recognition of the state by its neighbouring countries. Located in the Muslim heartland, Israel lacked legitimacy as a viable Jewish state. The first stage of bilateral talks started in Madrid in October 1991 and the second stage in mid-January 1992. The parties concentrated on procedural issues such as venue, format, and agenda.[19]

On 28 January 1992, the third stage of multilateral talks started. These talks dealt with region wide functional issues, which were carried on in five thematic groups and these groups met regularly to deal with these issues, they included the following:

a) Arms control and regional security

b) Water resources

c) The environment

d) Eeconomic growth

e) Refugees

Most of the world's leading powers were actively involved in multilateral talks,[20] like the US, Japan, and some West European countries.

Some Obstacles

In spite of all the efforts made to date, a number of obstacles remained. The issues which needed to be settled between Arab states and Israel, included: 1) sovereignty, 2) territory, 3) recognition of national rights, 4) the nature of peace. The Arab states involved in these issues are the following.

Jordan

King Hussein was committed to the peace process and to recognizing Israel. On 14 September 1993, Jordan and Israel signed an agenda of talks in Washington. On 25 July 1994, Jordan and Israel signed a non-belligerency pact at the White House in Washington D.C. On 17 October 1994, a peace treaty was signed between Jordan and Israel agreed to divert some 50 million cubic metres of water to Jordan. Jordan would be able to reassert its sovereignty over a piece of land measuring 380 square kilometres occupied by Israel. Jordan will lease part of it to Israel. The formal signing ceremony of the treaty took place on 26 October 1994. President Clinton attended the signing ceremony at the border crossing between Jordan and Israel. The peace treaty accorded Jordan a special role in supervising religious institutions in the disputed city of Jerusalem. The Palestinians agreed to defer their claims to East Jerusalem and put off negotiations on the status of the city for two years.

A clash erupted between Jordan and PLO over the control of Jerusalem's religious sites on 18 October 1994, when Arafat and King Hussein appointed two different Muftis in Jerusalem. Israel's affirmation of Jordan's special role in Jerusalem further aggravated the situation. Regarding militarization on the borders there is a *de facto* basis between Jordan and Israel. The Jordanian army is not a problem to Israel like the Egyptian or Syrian army, and it is small. The Jordanian borders will not be militarized by distant armies like Iraq's. Israel might need a *de jure* basis. Any violations will be considered *casus belli* for her.[21]

Syria

At the Madrid Conference, Syria entered into direct bilateral talks with Israel for the first time. Syria's main goal had been to regain control over the Golan Heights.

The conflict between Israel and Syria is about paragraph 5a of the agenda of talks, providing for a complete Israeli withdrawal from the Golan Heights, which was occupied in 1967 and a dismantling of all settlements which were established in occupied Syrian territories. Israel's answer would depend on the nature of peace to be engaged in by Syria.[22]

Israel may withdraw its army from the east and perhaps it would establish a buffer zone of 50-60 square kilometres, such as it had established with Egypt. This can be implemented through the UN disengagement warning stations on the other force. Each side can retain early warning stations on other's territories.[23]

Lebanon

Syria has a dominant position and influence over the Lebanese government. Lebanon and Israel have no territorial dispute. Lebanon wants Israel to withdraw from the southern security zone so that it could reassert its authority there. Israel expects from Lebanon the demilitarization of distant armies, such as the Syrian army, from the borders.

PLO

Although the PLO's position was different from other partners involved in the peace process, Israel and the US had a negative stand regarding the PLO. Israel banned contacts with the PLO. When direct talks started in Madrid in October 1991, Israel negotiated with Palestinian representatives. These representatives were technically part of the Jordanian-Palestinian delegation, but they were persona non grata to PLO. The Palestinian delegation to the Madrid Conference represented Palestinians from the occupied territories. In short, the PLO was excluded from the peace process. The Palestinian representatives from the occupied territories contacted PLO officials during the Madrid Conference in 1991 and then the talks shifted from Madrid to Washington, D.C. The Palestinian delegation publicly visited the PLO headquarter in Tunisia. Israel pretended to shut its eyes.[24] That contact was important as long as the Palestinian delegation did not recognize the PLO and the Palestinians living outside the occupied territories. The head of the Palestinian delegation to Madrid and Washington, Heider Abdel Shafi was of the view that PLO members could not play a part in inside affairs until it held democratic elections for the Palestininan National Council (PNC).[25] In 1992, the Israeli election were won by the Labour Party, which termed peace with the Arab world a national priority. The Israel Kenesset repealed the ban on contacts with PLO. Israel had already started confidential talks with the PLO before the ban was lifted. The talks started in Oslo (Norway) and ran parallel with the talks in Washington, D.C., which Israel conducted with the Palestinians representing the occupied territories. In these talks the PLO reduced its claims and accepted the proposal of interim self-rule before the initiation of talks on the ultimate sovereign status of the West Bank and the Gaza Strip.[26]

Purpose of Talks

Talks between Israel and the PLO aimed at forming a provisional Palestinian self-government body council in the West Bank for a transitional period of five years. This was in line with Security Council Resolutions 242 and 338, which called for a permanent settlement. On 13 September 1993, the two sides signed the Palestinian-Israeli Declaration of Principals in Washington. Israel was in an advantageous position because it had the opportunity to choose the best from among the insiders and the outsiders. The PLO allowed the formal talks over the status of Jerusalem to be delayed until as late as the spring of 1996. This was the single most important reason that Rabin shook hands with Arafat on 13 September 1993. The delegation from the territories refused to accept postponement of the Jerusalem question.[27] The treaty was signed in Washington, D.C., in the presence of the Israeli Premier Yitzhak Rabin, US President Bill Clinton, and PLO Chairman Yasser Arafat. It was signed by President Clinton, Israeli Foreign Minister Shimon Peres, and PLO executive committee members Mahmoud Abbas and Abu Mazen. The next day, on 14 September 1993, Jordan signed an agenda for talks with Israel. The PLO, which had rejected Camp David Accord in 1978, accepted less than that proposal had offered 15 years later.

Israeli Diplomacy

At first, Israel tried to have negotiations with the insiders and had formal bilateral talks with them. Later, however, it changed its strategy by having confidential bilateral talks with the outsiders. By having options open with each side, Israel got the best from the outsiders, that is the PLO.

A conflict started between PLO and Hammas, the holy Islamic movement which appeared in the Gaza Strip during late 1987. In the beginning, both Israel and the PLO considered Hammas a mystical band of talkers rather than doers.[29]

But after the Gulf crisis, Hammas attained a notable position especially when Saudi Arabia supported it financially to punish PLO Chairman Yasser Arafat for taking sides with Iraq in the crisis. Hammas has been quite influential in the Gaza Strip where the Palestinians numbered around 750,000, while in the West Bank where the number of Palestinians is 1.1 million the group has not been so effective.[30] Hammas is not regarded as a great threat for many reasons. For example, by 1992 Israel had deported more than 400 Hammas activists to the borders of Lebanon and ignored the UN resolution and pressure to promptly bring them back. Moreover, Hammas could not revert back to the most destructive practices of Haji Amin E.L. Huseini, who waged war against Palestinians and was suspected of collaborating with Israeli authorities, as these practices failed to entail the support of any Arab state. For instance, when Israel in the summer of 1994 accused Jordan of giving Hammas leaders some facilities for meeting and moving in Amman, Jordan declared that it would not do that anymore.

The future of Hammas is related to the toughness of the PLO Chairman Yasser Arafat, who is now caught in the middle, wedged between Israel's demands to crack down on the so-called Muslim fundamentalists who are responsible for deadly attacks against Israel, and the perception of his own people who believe that he has been too soft on Israel. On 3 November 1994, he was forced out of a mosque in Gaza by people who prevented him from saying prayers over the body of a Palestinian leader killed by a car bomb.

Future Trends

The prospects of a Middle East peace settlement depend on the economic development of the region which in the long run could reduce the chances of a military conflict between Israel and its adversaries.

The studies conducted in this connection also regard the economic development of the area as most vital for the success of the peace process. The idea of a regional bank for cooperation and development, recommended by Institute of Social and Economic Policy in the Middle East (IEPME), was also endorsed by the first Middle East-North Africa Economic Summit held in Casablanca (Morocco). The Summit decided to provide the much-needed help in technical Know-how for the setting up of the bank. According to one estimate more than 12 billion dollars are required for the setting up of the proposed bank over the next ten years.

A free trade area is expected between Jordan, Syria, Lebanon, and Israel. The success of all the economic plans depends on the progress of the peace process.

Conclusion

The aim of this paper as mentioned earlier has been to explore the constraints and capabilities of the Arab-Israeli peace process. Having done that one is bound to draw the following conclusions:

1. The constraints on the peace process were very effective during the period of 1948–1967. Formally, the Arab League passed two resolutions in 1950 that called for expulsion of any member state which made separate peace with Israel. In this connection, King

Abdullah of Jordan who had confidential talks with Israel, not only came under severe criticism but one year later was assassinated. Since then any hope of having a separate peace treaty with Israel disappeared. The Arab Demands during this period were to restore the land which had been occupied by Israel in 1948, and the only option available for the fulfillment of this demand appeared to be none other than war.

2. In 1967, Israel entered the third war against the Arabs and occupied the Golan Heights, Sinai, the West Bank, and the Gaza Strip. The security council Resolution 242 proposed a new formula for peace between Israel and the Arab states. By accepting this resolution, the Arab states abandoned the war option and decided to initiate dialogue for the realization of their demands.

3. Resolution 242 was interpreted differently by the two sides as each argued over the word "territories." Each side adopted a different point of view. The political situation remained frozen until the 1973 war created a better political climate for peace. Security Council Resolution 242 was reaffirmed by Resolution 338. This resolution led to the Geneva Conference which Syria declined to take part in.

4. After the 1973 war, the American administration became more active in resolving the Arab-Israel conflict; for instance, during the period 1973–1975, three agreements were signed between Syria, Egypt, and Israel. Carter's Administration followed the same course of action with regard to the Arab-Israel conflict, and it was during the same administration that Israel and Egypt concluded the Camp David Accord in 1979.

5. American efforts continued in the following years. President Reagan, having failed to extract concessions from PLO, tried to have peace with the Palestinians living in the West Bank and the Gaza Strip. Although the PLO made a clear concession and accepted the Resolution 242, it was excluded and did not participate in the Madrid Conference.

Israel took advantage of this situation and started confidential talks with PLO in parallel with talks in Washington, D.C., with the Palestinian representatives from the occupied territories. The PLO made concessions to Israel and allowed talks on the status of Jerusalem to be delayed until as late as the spring of 1996. PLO Chairman Arafat has been caught in a dilemma as Israel has asked him to crack down on the so-called Muslim fundamentalists while the Palestinians accuse him of being too soft on Israel. The fear of civil war arose between Arafat's supporters and his Islamic rivals.

There are still many things to be settled like water distribution, status of Jerusalem, and armament. There are no signs that the Arab diplomacy could get more from Israel.

The American administration must be given credit for having worked all these years for a Middle East peace settlement and having brought the adversaries to the negotiating table. The Middle East peace process has worked to the advantage of Israel since it succeeded in getting from Arabs what it had always wanted. In the prevailing circumstances, the Arabs could not have got from Israel a better deal.

Notes

1. See in detail, Dorhout, Aneta M, "American Israeli Relations during the Nixon Administration 1969–1974." (USA: San Jose State University, M.A. Dissertation, 1993).

2. Alfred Atherton, "The Shifting Sands of Middle East Peace," *Foreign Policy* (Washington, D.C.), No. 86 (Spring 1992), p.115; Alfred el Khazen, "The Middle East in Strategic Retreat," *Foreign Policy*, No. 64, (Fall 1986), p.157.

3. The Iraq-Iran war started when the Iraqi soldiers crossed the borders of Iran on 22 September 1980; the Iraqi President, Saddam Hussein, was poorly advised by the Iranian Resistance leaders and other Arab leaders.

4. See Alan Kreezko, "Support Reagan's Initiative," *Foreign Policy*, No. 49 (Winter, 1982–1983), pp. 140-155; Winslow Richard Lawrence, *American Military Intervention in the Middle East*: In a few weeks, he could neutralize the Iranian Revolution, led by Ayotallah Khomeine, who denounced the Algiers Accord as an American conspiracy between the ex-Shah of Iran and Iraq. See Nita M. Renfrew, "Who Stated the War," *Foreign Policy*, Vol.66, (Spring 1987), p. 98. The Iraqi-Irani roots go back to 1947, when the Treaty of Erzurum was signed between the Ottoman and Persian governments. Since then, the Ottomans had the right to control the whole Shatt-Al-Arab, the 50-mile channel which is constituted by the confluence of the Tigris and Euphrates. In 1913, the Persian frontiers were demarcated according to the protocol signed in Constantinople. In 1914, a demarcation committee was

formed. But after the Second World War, Reza Shah pressed for a revision of the 1847 treaty. He wanted to have an Iranian oil terminal free from Iraqi control. British diplomacy was able to make the two sides reach a new agreement in 1937. In the late fifties, after the collapse of the monarchy in Iraq, the dispute appeared again, and Security Council Resolution No. 348 was issued in 1974 to settle the dispute. In 1975, the Algerian diplomacy made the two sides sign a treaty on 13 June 1975, which provided for:

1) Delimitation of their frontiers on the basis of Constantinople Protocol and the records of Borders Demarcation Commission of 1914.

2) Definition of water boundaries on the basis of the lweg Line.

3) The re-establishment of security and mutual confidence. This item helped Iraq reach an agreement with the Kurds whom Iraq stopped supporting. In 1980, Iraq declared the treaty to be null and void. See Hussein Siriyeh, "The Iraqi-Iranian Dispute," *Journal of Contemporary History*, Vol. 20, (1985), pp. 483-492.

Political Prudence, Military Feasibility and Moral Permissibility: An analysis of four cases, Vol. I and II (Georgetown University, PhD Dissertation, 1989).

5. Kreezko, op.cit., pp. 140-155.

6. Hasan Bin Talal, "Return to Geneva," *Foreign Policy* No.57, (1984–1985), pp. 8-13.

7. Jim, Lederman, "Dateline West Bank: Interpreting the Intifada," *Foreign Policy* Vol. 72, (Fall 1988), pp. 243-230, 232-234.

8. Ibid., pp. 230-234.

9. Daniel Williams, "Dateline Tunis PLO R.I.P.," *Foreign Policy*, No.90 (Spring 1993), p. 162.

10. See Luti William, "Ends Versus Means: A Critical Analysis of the Persian Gulf Crisis 1987–1988, Kuwait-Iraq-Iran." (USA: Fletcher School of Law and Diplomacy: Tufts University, PhD Disseration, 1991).

11. Philip Matter, "The Critical Moment for Peace," *Foreign Policy*, Vol.76 (Fall 1989), p. 141; Robert Hunter, "Seeking Middle East Peace," *Foreign Policy*, Vol. 73 (Winter 1968-1969), p. 21.

12. Although the Iraqi President argued that Iraq had a historical basis to its claim to Kuwait, there were other motives as well and he demanded compensation for Kuwait's exploitation of transborder oil fields and the remission of loans granted during the Iraq-Iran war. Iraq's debt after the war was

around US\$ 70 Billion. Negotiations started between Iraq and its small neighbour Kuwait. After the first round the Iraqi invasion started, Iraq expected that it could gain control over the oil fields, to become the most powerful in the oil cartel OPEC. See Ursula Braun, "Epicenter Kuwait the International Political Dimension of a Religious Conflict" in *Aussen Politik*, Vol.42, pp. 42.

13. Atherton, op. cit., pp. 58-67.

14. Allexei Thistiakov, "Changes in the Middle East and the Outside World," in *Gorokhousky Peeulok* (Moscow), p. 108.

15. Ibid.

16. Atherton, op. cit., p. 130.

17. Ibid.

18. Thistiakoy, op. cit., p. 110.

19. Joseph Alpher, "Israel's Security Concerns in the Peace Process," *International Affairs*, Vol. 70, No.2, (1994), pp. 229-230.

20. Ibid., p. 232. The study refers to the real threat which in the Israelis' consideration, was an Arab attack. A Jaffee Centre Survey, conducted in January 1993, found that 85 percent of the Israelis feared attack by the Arabs.

21. Ibid., p. 229.

22. Ibid., p. 236.

23. Thistiakov, op. cit., p. 108.

24. Alpher, op.cit., p. 234.

25. Williams, op.cit., p. 163,

26. Ibid., p. 165.

27. Ibid., p. 163.

28. Ian Lustick, "Reinventing," *Foreign Policy*, No.93, (Winter 1993–1994).

29. Williams, op.cit., p. 165.

30. Ibid., p. 166.

CHAPTER 12

Japan's Foreign Policy toward the Arab World in the 1990s: The Post Cold War Era, Gulf Crisis, and Peace Process

Abstract

The purpose of this study is to examine the new trends of Japan's foreign policy in the Arab World in the 1990 and to explore Japan's new role after the dramatic changes which took place in the 1990s, like the end of the Cold War, the Gulf Crisis which was the first crisis after the end of the Cold War, and the peace developments between the Arab world and the Israelis after the Madrid Conference. This paper explores the constraints on and capabilities of Japan's foreign policy toward the Arab World in the period 1990–1995. Historically, the US sought to rebuild Japan into a strong ally in the Cold War against the U.S.S.R. Japan was accused to taking advantage of the US policy of containment to protect its interests and to secure its access to foreign markets. Contrary to this traditional idea, we found that there is a limit to the American pressure on Japan. Japan had its own diplomacy on many occasions and expected to have a new role in the 1990s commensurate with its economical role.

There are constraints on the new role by western countries and Asian neighbors, and there is a fear that Japan is becoming too powerful a country and will repeat the experience of the thirties and forties. However, there is no such fear in the Middle East, and there are no negative feeling nor any psychological barriers between the Japanese and the Arabs. The two sides can complete with each other. This study revealed the constraints on and capabilities of Japan foreign policy in the Middle East prime issues like the Gulf Crisis and peace process.

The Gulf Crisis is a vivid example of the pressure on Japan to play new role outside of financial support. There are variables which constrained Japan's foreign policy in the Gulf Crisis. In the Gulf Crisis, Japan strived for diplomatic autonomy, and tried to maintain a balance between the two side in any conflict. This policy was much clearer in the Arab-Israeli conflict.

The main constraints on Japanese foreign policy toward Israel, during the Cold War was exercised by Arabs. After the peace process, Japan played an active role in the peace process between the two sides. Japan participated in the multilateral track of the peace process between Israel and its neighbors.

The role of Japan in the Gulf Crisis was wider than it has ever been. In the two cases, Japan played new role within the traditional role of Japan international behavior to give priority to economic growth over political leadership. In general, the government of Japan is operating under political constraints mostly domestic and economical. Both are capabilities of Japan foreign policy toward the Arab world.

Historical Sketch about the American Influence on Japan Foreign Policy

Because of Japan's geostrategic importance between the two superpowers, the US and the U.S.S.R. during the Cold War, Japan relied heavily on the US, which sought to rebuild Japan into a strong ally in the Cold War against the U.S.S.R. Many studies reflected the same idea that Japan's foreign policy after the Second World War was subordinated to the US and Japan didn't have its own diplomatic autonomy. Japan was accused of taking advantage of the US policy containment to protect its interests, and to secure its access to foreign markets.

The American Influence and the Arab Israeli Conflict

In the Arab Israeli Conflict, Japan gave priority to its own interest and regardless of the American position, Japanese companies avoided any direct contact with Israel until 1989 when ten companies were established in Israel by Japan.[1]

(1) Economically, the Japanese companies adopted an attitude of deliberately avoiding direct business contact with Israeli firms.[2]

(2) So, the main constraints on Japanese foreign policy toward Israel during the Cold War was by Arabs. Any American influence was not effective.

The New Role of Japan in the 1990s

When the Gulf Crisis started in 1990 and when the peace process took place between Israel and the Arabs in 1991, Japan was expected to have a high international profile,[3] and to have a new sense of international responsibility[4] and to leave the neutralist tendencies that prevailed during the Cold War especially after its economy revived beyond all expectations.[5] In any event, Japan must have a new global political role commensurate with its economical role.[6]

The Constraints on the New Role of Japan

There are constraints on the new role of Japan by western countries and Asian[7] neighbors, who fear that Japan is becoming too powerful a country and that it will repeat the experience of the thirties and forties, or fear that Japan role will be on their expense. However, in the Middle East, there is no fear that Japan will cause political or economical hardships. Moreover, there are no memories of the Second World War among the Arabs against Japan, and there is no negative feeling nor any psychological barriers between Japanese and the Arabs.[8] So any role of Japan toward the Arab World doesn't need changes at home in Japan, and the Japanese domestic influence won't be a barrier. The two sides can complete with each other.

The New Role and the Gulf Crisis in 1990

The Gulf Crisis started in 1990 and created a problem for Japan, which depends on Mideast oil as primary source of energy. In Japan, the argument arose that Japan must stay completely out of the conflict to secure its economic interest. Japan receives 55% of its oil from the Gulf states. Any decision would be very difficult. In spite of that, Japan made the difficult decision to join the western powers. The decision of Japan followed the European Community decision of August 4th, 1990, to impose trade sanctions against Iraq.[9]

Japan banned Iraqi and Kuwaiti oil imports and blocked Japanese exports to those countries, suspended all capital transactions and forze aid to Iraq. The decision was hard on Japan which imported 12% of its oil supply from Kuwait and Iraq.[10]

The American Influence in the Gulf Crisis

In the Gulf Crisis, Japan's choice was limited. The U.S. acted as the hegemonic leader and led the international coalition against Iraq. Japan couldn't play the role it wanted to play. Although in some occasions, Japan's foreign policy appeared very close to the western countries. In the Iran-Iraq war and contrary to the official position of Japan not to get entangled by any side in the war, Japan acted politically the same as the western powers. It went further and served with Algeria and Switzerland as an intermediary between the US and Iran to free the western hostages in the early 1990s.[11] In some other occasions Japan has its own diplomacy. For example, Japan didn't condemn Iran when the international furor in 1989 continued against the Iranian President Khamenei who condemned Salman Rushdie for his *Satanic Verses* book.[12] Moreover, Japan refused to send the mine sweepers to the Gulf when the tanker war started between Iran and Iraq in 1987.[13]

In short, Japan had its diplomacy during the war between Iran and Iraq, but Japan could not repeat the same role again in the Gulf Crisis in 1990. The criticism became greater than it was in 1987.[14]

The Pressures on Japan in the Gulf Crisis

Japan was under external and internal pressure[15] during the Gulf Crisis. The blame was from both sides. The U.S. wanted Japan to have a military role in the crisis. Japan didn't welcome any military role. In general, Japan international behavior gave priority to economic growth over political or military leadership.[16] Moreover, there was domestic pressure on the Japanese government not to join any combat in the Gulf. Japan's consitution prohibited any direct involvement in overseas combat activities. A poll conducted in December 1990 found that 62% of those Japanese questioned opposed any involvement in the Gulf efforts outside of financial support.[17]

Japan Deployment

The Japanese cabinet on Oct. 16th, 1990, approved a plan to send non-combat soldiers, about 1,000 members of Japan Armed Forces, known as the Self Defense Forces (SDF), to Saudia Arabia. However, Prime Minister Kaifu faced criticism by his people for his eagerness to please the U.S. President George Bush. The socialist Party leader Takako Doi, on Oct. 16th, vowed to fight the proposal and accused the premier that he was asking the youth of Japan to shed blood on a battlefield.

More Domestic and External Pressure

The proposal was opposed not by the opposition party but by the Japanese public[18] who disapproved the plan by a two-to-one margin according to opinion surveys. Government officials were cautious that the proposal would demonstrate Japanese support for the efforts against Iraq. Even the Asian neighbors expressed strong reservation against the plan. Japan's ruling Liberal Democratic Party (LDP) on Nov. 10th, 1990, formally withdrew the proposal.

Financial Support and Domestic Pressure in the Gulf Crisis

Trying to avoid an involvement in combat, Japan insisted on providing only financial support. On Jan. 17th, 1991, Japanese Prime Minister Toshiki Kaifu said that his nation would extend the maximum support possible for allied military action but wouldn't join the combat effort. Japan promised further financial aid to the allied effort. It pledged $9 Billion dollars in new aid to fund the war effort. The total amount by the end of January 1991 was $13 Billion, which meant 1/5 of the amount that had been spent on the crisis until then. The opposition party demanded that any funding must be devoted to non-combat operations. The Japanese public worries increased.[19] The domestic pressure effectively constrained Japanese foreign policy toward any form of military participation. When Prime Minister Toshiki Kaifu proposed on Jan. 24th, 1991, that Japan sent non-combat aircraft to the Gulf to help evacuate the refugees from the area, the opposition was very strong from within the ruling Liberal Democratic Party (LDP) and from opposition politicians.

What made the Japanese worry more about deploying aircraft to the region was the Iraqi ambassador to Japan, who said that any military aircraft operating in the area would be subject to attack.[20] Japan was already was reluctant to use any military force or to get entangled in the Gulf Crisis. The constitution of Japan forbade the use of the military for non-defensive purposes. The Japanese regarded this constitution as a guarantee that the nationalistic militarism of the 1930s and 1940s wouldn't be repeated. The domestic opinion opposed the decision to attack Iraq. According to public survey, the Japanese public was against attacking Iraq. So more pressure went on the measures which were proposed by Prime Minister Kaifu to help fund the Gulf Crisis.[21]

Criticism of Japan

Japan strove for diplomatic autonomy in the Gulf Crisis. The official position was not to get entangled by in that war. Although in some cases Japan acted politically the same way as western powers, Japan tried to avoid direct involvement as much as possible. But the criticism increased. Although Japan's contributions to the Gulf Crisis costs were very high, criticism against Japan continued. Japan's contribution to the Gulf War wasn't fully appreciated because of the slowness with which it was offered. And Japan was criticized for its reluctance to provide any personnel and was charge of hiring mercenaries to fight for its interests.[22] Japan did its best to avoid participating in any combat in the Gulf Crisis. In spite of the high percentage of Japan contributions to the Crisis cost, the criticism continued in many forms. The criticism came from the press and from formal figures. There was a great criticism that Japan's contribution in the international efforts in the Gulf Crisis was insufficient. Japan was accused of sending only shipments of goods consisting of 800 vehicles of the original one billion aid pledge for the Gulf. Moreover, Japan was accused of recruiting only three doctors[23] for a 100-member medical unit that had been pledged for the Gulf. More criticism to Japan by congress members for a lack of cooperation in the Gulf efforts. The house, on Sept. 12th, 1990, passed an Authorization Bill calling for Japan to assume the entire cost of basing 50,000 U.S. troops in Japan. If Japan didn't pick up the cost, the amendment called for 5,000 troops a year to be withdrawn.[24] When George Bush addressed the joint session of Congress on Sept. 11th, 1990, the House majority leader Richard Gephardt criticized Japan.

Dan Quayle, who was visiting Japan on May 21st, 1991, urged Japan to pay the difference of the exchange rate between the dollar and yen, which was half a billion dollars, and which led to a friction between Japan and U.S. In December 1991, Japan, among other countries, was accused of supporting the Iraqi weapons projects. The report, which was released by the International Atomic Energy Agency on Dec. 11th, 1991, revealed the names of the companies who sold equipment to Iraq for use in clandestine efforts to develop atomic weapons.[25] Japan was expected to pay more of the cost of the crisis. When England declared in July 1991 that its cost in the Persian Gulf was $ 4.15 Billion, Japan was expected to pay it with Saudi Arabia, UAE, and Kuwait.[26]

Japan's Participation after the Cease Fire in the Gulf

The public opinion in Japan changed after the ceasefire, and it supported the decision to send Japanese tankers to the Gulf. Japan could participate in the Allied effort and the participation was justified to clear the explosives on the grounds; Japanese tankers traveled the Persian Gulf. Public opinion supported the decision because the mission was regarded as safe.

Helping Refugees

The Japanese government showed other interest and contributed on 24th, April 1991, with an additional $82.5 Million for emergency relief for refugees from Iraq. Two days later, Japan pledged $100 Million to the office of the UN High Commissioner to help Kurdish refugees.

The Diplomacy of Japan

Trying to avoid the turmoil in the Middle East, Japanese Prime Minister Kaifu canceled a planned trip to the region. But later, to avoid the complaints from the US and its allies that Japan wasn't doing enough to assist the Gulf efforts, Kaifu visited Jordan on Oct. 4th, and met with Iraqi deputy premier Taha Yasin Ramadan, who refused to negotiate as long as foreign troops remained on Arab soil. Kaifu insisted on an Iraqi withdrawal from Kuwait first.[27]

The Position of Iraq toward Japan

Iraq treated Japan like western countries, who defied Iraq to keep their missions open. On 24th August 1990, Iraqi troops surrounded nine embassies, including the Japanese embassy. And when Iraq held hostages, there were 500 Japanese among the 9,600 western foreigners.[28] But when the former Japanese Prime Minister Yasuhiro Nakasone visited Baghdad on Nov. 4, 1990, and met with Iraqi President Saddam Hussein twice, he obtained the release of 74 Japanese.[29] Japan tried to avoid any military role and offered covering the losses sustained because of the crisis, and volunteered to offer compensation to the Arab states who were hurt economically by the UN trade embargo of Iraq. Japan promised to send medical personnel and some supplies to the US-led Gulf forces.[30] On August 29, 1990, Japan unveiled a package of economic and logistical contributions to the international efforts. On the 30th, Japan declared the package would be worth $1 Billion.[31]

On Nov. 10th, 1990, and after the LDP and opposition leaders reached and agreement to send civilian medical technical personnel to the Gulf, the Japanese team of seven doctors and nurses who went to Saudi Arabia returned home.[32]

A poll conducted in December opposed any further involvement in the Gulf Crisis outside of financial support.[33] There were political constraints under which the government of Japan was operating. Japanese resisted any military entanglements and refused to send members of SDF abroad in combat roles even as members of the UN peace-keeping operation.

Peacekeeping Force

It took a long time for the Japanese Diet Parliament to agree on a bill which allowed up to 2,000 personnel to be dispatched abroad to participate in UN peace-keeping missions. The US, however, was critical of Japan's motives, and accused Japan of practicing "checkbook diplomacy"—a willingness to pay for international peace-keeping operation, but not to support them with personnel.

The scope of Japan's participation was limited. The legislation of 1992 permitted a small number at armed forces to be dispatched abroad, but not for the threat or use of force. This policy was fully compatible with the constitution which forbade the use of the military for non-defensive purposes.

Among the restrictive clauses was a limit on the forces' weaponry to small sidearms. The forces were authorized to go to a region where a cease fire had been declared but had to evacuate the area if the ceasefire was broken.

Japan and the Arab Israeli Conflict

The Arab Israeli conflict was a sensitive issue to Japan which tried to maintain a balance between the two sides; for example, when Japan's Prime Minister Toshiki Kaifu received PLO Chairman Yasir Arafat on Oct. 3rd, 1989, the following month he received the Israeli foreign minister.[34]

Japan's dependence on Middle East oil as a primary source of energy was inescapable. In 1985, Japanese imports of oil were 91%, which reflected an excessive dependence on Middle East oil as the primary source of energy. This was one of the main constraints on Japan's diplomacy in the Middle East. Japan couldn't respond like the US by using a military rapid-deployment force for times of crisis.[35]

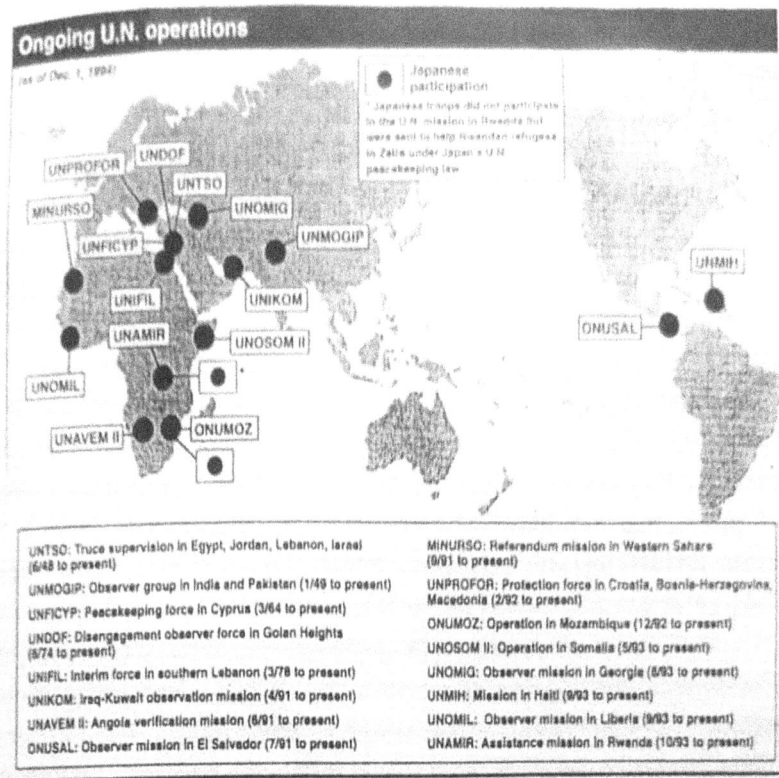

Ongoing U.N. operations

(as of Dec. 1, 1994)

Japanese participation

Japanese troops did not participate in the U.N. mission in Rwanda but were sent to help Rwandan refugees in Zaïre under Japan's U.N. peacekeeping law.

UNTSO: Truce supervision in Egypt, Jordan, Lebanon, Israel (6/48 to present)

UNMOGIP: Observer group in India and Pakistan (1/49 to present)

UNFICYP: Peacekeeping force in Cyprus (3/64 to present)

UNDOF: Disengagement observer force in Golan Heights (6/74 to present)

UNIFIL: Interim force in southern Lebanon (3/78 to present)

UNIKOM: Iraq-Kuwait observation mission (4/91 to present)

UNAVEM II: Angola verification mission (6/91 to present)

ONUSAL: Observer mission in El Salvador (7/91 to present)

MINURSO: Referendum mission in Western Sahara (9/91 to present)

UNPROFOR: Protection force in Croatia, Bosnia-Herzegovina, Macedonia (2/92 to present)

ONUMOZ: Operation in Mozambique (12/92 to present)

UNOSOM II: Operation in Somalia (5/93 to present)

UNOMIG: Observer mission in Georgia (8/93 to present)

UNMIH: Mission in Haiti (9/93 to present)

UNOMIL: Observer mission in Liberia (9/93 to present)

UNAMIR: Assistance mission in Rwanda (10/93 to present)

SOURCE : FOREIGN MINISTRY

Japan and the Peace Talks

After the Madrid Conference and the new developments in the Middle East peace talks, it was expected that Japan would seek a wider role in achieving a lasting peace, both diplomatically and economically and to strengthen its relations with both Israel and Arab Nations.[36]

For the first time in the Arab-Israeli conflict, Japan joined the peace talks. It was expected that Japan was seeking a wider role in diplomacy in the Middle East.[37] Japan's role in the bilateral and multilateral talks was clear. Japan was now participating in the multilateral working group on the environment. Japan was a major partner in the working groups for regional economic development and water source development.

Japan was expected to play an active role in strengthening relations between Israel and its neighbors because it was a joint organizer of the multilateral track of the peace process. Although Japan's limited role in the multilateral talks was clear, Israel sought Japan's economic assistance, which would help people in the region feel that peace has as really come. Israel demanded assistance from Japan to overcome poverty, which creates fertile grounds for the growth of Hammas and the Islamic Jihad.[38]

The Israeli Prime Minister tried to motivate the Japanese directly and indirectly, arguing that Israel would be the regional center for commerce and industry, and that Israel and Japan could complement each other instead of working parallel in the same area.[39]

It was expected that the conflict between Israel and the Arab World put a constraint on Japan's foreign policy. The first visit of the Israeli Prime Minister to Japan didn't reflect any of new trends in Japan's foreign policy toward Israel, however. What the Israeli Prime Minister got were two pacts: the science and technology cooperation pact, which was the first that Japan concluded with any Middle Eastern country was the second after that had with Egypt.[40]

Japan is still reluctant to get entangled in any conflict. Peace in the Middle East is still in its beginnings. Israel still occupies Golan Heights and south Lebanon. This made Japan oppose sending a fact-finding mission to Golan Heights to weigh possible Japanese assistance in the UN peacekeeping operating there. The cabinet showed much caution against this suggestion; Japanese officials expressed their concern about Japanese participation in UNDOF on the grounds that the operation, unlike the other UN missions in which Japan has participated so far, will probably be extended over a long time. One of the officials expressed the concern in another way. He said, "It is wrong for the Foreign Ministry to think it is taken for granted that personnel can be sent whenever requested (by the UN)."[41]

In general, Japan is still hesitant to deal with Israel. Japan is committed to five multilateral working groups that have been meeting in tandem with bilateral talks between Israel and the Arab states.[42]

Psychological Barriers

Japan's caution might be related to economical and psychological reasons. With respect to the future, Japanese-Arab relations are promising. If the peace works out, it will be no problem for Japan to deal with the Middle East. There is a large market in the Arab world and there are not any psychological barriers between the Japanese and Arabs. The Arabs have no negative feeling toward Japanese and Arabs have no negative memories of Japanese activities during the Second World War, unlike the Koreans or Chinese, for example. But it must be mentioned that Japanese people have negative feelings toward Jewish people. This is largely attributable to the influence of books, ranging from *The Merchant of Venice* by Shakespeare to anti-Semitic books written by Masami Uno.[43]

Nobuo Fujiwara, president of the Japan-Israel Culture and Business Association, which was established in April 1994, said "Israel has a completely different culture and by acknowledging the difference we will be able to improve relations for the first time."[44]

To summarize what has been said we can mention the following:

- The peace process accomplishments in 1993–1994 didn't affect Japanese diplomacy in the Middle East. The Japanese commitment is within the framework of the five multilateral working groups that have been meeting in tandem with the bilateral talks taking place between Israel and the Arab states.

- If the peace process doesn't work out, this will not be to the advantage of Israel. Japan was reluctant to deal with Israel during the conflict. Since the peace process started, Japan has a new role for the first time. Japan committed $200 Million in aid over two years to help implement the peace process. In the region following the September 1993 Agreement between PLO and Israel, Japan spent $10 million in housing for families of Palestinian police officers. Japan expected to establish social infrastructure such as hospitals and schools in the West Bank and Gaza Strip. Diplomatically, after Rabin's visit to Japan, Japan Prime Minister Murayama promised that Japan would call on Syria to make greater efforts to establish peaceful relations with the Jewish state.

Japan's foreign policy continued to be balanced between Israel and Arab states. For example, when Rabin asked Japan to open an office of the Japan External Trade Organization in Israel to facilitate business activities, Mr. Ryutaro Hashimoto, Minister of International Trade and Industry, answered that it was too difficult to open an office in Israel because of the nation's tight fiscal conditions. He took a balanced position and suggested that M.I.T. invite trainees from Israel the following month under a two-week training program aimed at providing know-how to the Middle East on promoting development of small and medium size firms. Other participants—Jordanians, Palestinians, and Egyptians—might be invited. Another example of this even-handed policy by Japan is Murayama's response to Rabin. When the latter asked for assistance for the Palestine authority in the Gaza Strip and the West Bank town of Jericho, Murayama responded that Japan would continue to provide assistance to the Palestine Authority in the area as well as to Israel's neighboring nations.[45] Japan took into consideration the small population of Israel.

A Conclusion and Future Trends

The purpose of this study is to examine the new trends of Japan's foreign policy in the Arab world in 1990, and to explore Japan's new role after the dramatic changes which took place in the 1990s like the end of the Cold War, the Gulf Crisis which was the first crisis after the end of the Cold War, and the peace developments between the Arab world and the Israelis after the Madrid Conference. This paper explored the constraints on and capabilities of Japan's foreign policy toward the Arab world in the period from 1990–1995. Historically, the US sought to rebuild Japan into a strong ally in the Cold War against the U.S.S.R. Japan was accused of taking advantage of the US policy containment to protect its interests and to secure its access to foreign markets. Contrary to this traditional idea, we found that there is a limit to American pressure on Japan. Japan had its own diplomacy on many occasions and expected to have a new role in the 1990s commensurate with its economical role.

There are constraints on Japan's the new role by western countries and Asian neighbors, and there is fear that Japan is becoming too powerful a country and it could repeat the experience of the 1930s and '40s. However, there is no such fear in the Middle East, and there are no negative feelings nor any psychological barriers between the Japanese and the Arabs. The two sides can work together.

This study revealed the constraints on and capabilities of Japan's foreign policy in the Middle East on prime issues like the Gulf Crisis and the peace process. The Gulf Crisis is a vivid example of the pressure on Japan to play new role outside of financial support. There are variables which constrained Japan's foreign policy in the Gulf Crisis. Japan strove for diplomatic autonomy and tried to maintain a balance between the two sides. This policy was much clearer in the Arab-Israeli conflict.

The main constraints on Japanese foreign policy toward Israel during the Cold War was exercised by Arabs. After the peace process, Japan played an active role in the peace process between the two sides. Japan participated in the multilateral track of the peace process between Israel and its neighbors.

The role of Japan in the Gulf Crisis was wider than it has ever been. In the two cases, Japan played a new role in international behavior to give priority to economic growth over political leadership. In general, the government of Japan is operating under political constraints mostly domestic and economic. Both of them are capabilities of Japan's foreign policy toward the Arab world.

At present there are three great economic powers in the world: the US, Europe, and Japan. These powers all have ties with the Arab world. Among them, Japan's ties are the weakest in the Arab world, despite its dependence on Arab oil. In the past and during the Cold War, Japan depended heavily on the US to secure its interests in the Arab world. But now, there are some indicators that reflect that Japan has other priorities in its diplomacy.

Relations with the US are no longer top priority. Japan has a priority now to strengthen ties with other Asian nations. Contribution to the UN is another priority. In general, some trends now reflect that Japan does not have the same old interest of maintaining solid ties with the US. Some writings reflect that Japan is fed up with US pressure and Japanese concessions in the bilateral talks.[46] Some commentators are pessimistic that Japan will have an economic Cold War with the US.[47] Others are more pessimistic to the degree that they expect that Japan will take over America economically by the end of this century.[48]

However, these studies often overestimate Japan's future. For example, studies in the seventies mistakenly predicted that Japan would be a nuclear state by the eighties.[49]

To be objective, it is true that Japan is the first example in the history of a state wielding huge economic and technological power with corresponding political or military might. And it is true that Japan is the third largest exporter of manufactured goods, the second largest contributor to the UN budget and to the World Bank,[50] and the largest donor of foreign aid in the last three years.[51]

We can argue that the role does not relate only to economic capabilities Japan needs to participate in political institutions. There are 150 plus slots allocated to Japan in the UN secretariat; only 88 are filled.

Accordingly, some analyst confusion still exists over Japan's policy on participation in UN missions. There is no clear international consensus on the distinction between the military and non- military activities of the UN. Under present law, Japanese participation is limited to non-combat activities. The troops are sent to sweat and not to bleed. If any Japanese are killed, the government will be thrown into confusion. This happened in the spring of 1993 when a Japanese volunteer was killed in Cambodia.[52]

Inside Japan, the government and people are not ready to commit themselves to a larger international role. It is widely expected that Japan's political instability will last another couple of years. The government has been reshuffled three times in the past 18 months.

In short, Japan has failed to make clear what new roles it can or wants to play as a permanent council member for the sake of global peace and prosperity leading into the 21st century.[53] Moreover, outside Japan there has been little support for a Japanese role in the UN; although the US officially supported the Japanese role in UN, it did little to advance it. France and the UK are resisting any expansion of Japan's role, expecting that it would be at their own expense, or will open the door to other countries.[54]

It looks clear that new trends are emerging between Japan and her Asian neighbors. Some of them have put aside what happened 50 years ago.[55] These neighbors have growing economic possibilities which attract Japan's attention.[56] This trend looks the strongest among Japan's foreign policy priorities; next autumn, Japan will host a summit of the leaders from the 18-member Asia-Pacific Economic Cooperation Forum. Moreover, Japan's concentration is on the regional grouping of ASEAN Members Brunei, Indonesia, Philippines, Singapore, and Thailand, which put together are a more prosperous population than all of Latin America and import more agricultural and industrial good from the US than the latter. In the year 2000, it is expected that two-thirds of the world's manufacturing capabilities will be located in this region. Since half of these ASEAN countries are Islamic (Indonesia, Brunei, and Malaysia), their growing ties with Japan may bridge the gap between Japan and the rest of the Islamic or Arab world.

In the 1995 budget, Japan aimed to construct deeper relationships with other Asian countries. Eight point two billion yen have been earmarked for this purpose.

Asia is the priority which Japan concentrates on now. This will be the major thrust of Japanese foreign policy toward the Arab world in the current circumstances of peace in East and West Asia. If there is change in these peaceful and economically profitable circumstances, Japanese foreign policy will take into revert to its old priority of ties with the US.

Notes

1. Statement by Raoji Tateyama, chief economist at the Japan Institute of Middle East Studies. See *Japan Times*, Dec.13, 1994.

2. Japanese foreign policy toward Vietnam was another example of the limit of American influence on Japan.

3. Forsberg, Aaron Patrick, *America and Resurgence of Post War Japan after the Occupation* (Economy Recovery, United States) (Austin, The University of Texas, PhD, 1993).

4. Funahashi, Yoichi, "Japan and America: Global Partners," *Foreign Policy*, 86, Spring 1992, p. 32.

5. Ibid.

6. See: A) Eugne Brown, "Japanese Security Policy in the post-cold war Era: Threat perceptions and Strategic Options," in *Asian Survey*, Vol XXXIV No.5 May 1994, p. 438.

7. Joseph S. Nye, Jr. "Coping with Japan," *Foreign Policy*, Winter 92-93, p. 108.

8. Nye, op.cit., pp.108, 110, 111.

9. An interview with Nobuo Fujiwara, President of Japan-Israel Culture and Business Association, wrote about the psychological barriers between Japan and Israel. See *Japan Times*, Dec. 13, 1994.

10. FACTS ON FILE (FOF), August 10th, 1990 (World News Digest with Index published weekly by Facts on File Inc. 460 Park Avenue South, New York, N.Y. 10016).

11. FOF August 10, 1990.

12. FOF May 4, 1990; FOF Dec. 19, 1986.

13. FOF Sept. 16, 1988; FOF Feb. 17, 1989. By then Japan was accused of being involved of shipment of US arms to Iran. Although Japanese Foreign Minister Nakasone admitted that he had spoken with President Regan, he denied any role in the subsequent shipment of US arms to Iran. Five years later, the Japan Aviation Electronic Industry Ltd. was convicted in a court in Tokyo of illegally exporting US-made missile components. The President and his officials were sentenced to prison and fined 5 million yen. See FOF April 30, 1994.

14. FOF Sept. 4, 1987.

15. President Regan blamed Germany and Japan in 1987 for not taking the initiative. Japan avoided the criticism by increasing the financial support to the American military presence in Japan and increasing its foreign aid to some Arab countries. See FOF Sept. 4, 1987; FOF Sept..7,1987.

16. Thomas M. Berger, "From Sword to Chrysanthemum: Japan's Culture of Anti Militarism," in *International Security* Vol. 17, No. 4, Spring 1993, p. 119.

17. Teab Saeed, *Role of Japan's Oil Industry and Emergence of Japan as a World Leader* (Hawaii University of Hawaii, PhD Dissertation, 1993).

18. FOF Jan. 10,1991.

19. Peter J. Katzenstein and Nobuo Okawara, "Japan's National Security: Structures, Norms, and Polices," *International Security*, Vol. 17, No. 4, Spring 1993, p. 109.

20. FOF Jan. 10,1991; FOF Jan. 17, 1991; FOF Jan. 24 1991; FOF Jan. 24, 1991; FOF Jan, 24, 1991.

21. FOF Jan. 24, 1991.

22. FOF Jan, 24, 1991.

23. Nye, op. cit., p. 108.

24. FOF Sept, 4, 1990.

25. *The Washington Post*, Sept. 9, 1990.

26. FOF Dec. 19, 1991; FOF May 25, 1991.

27. FOF May 25, 1991.

28. FOF August 24, 1990. And see Koji Watanabe "Challenges and opportuni-

ties for the Japanese diplomacy-Gulf Crisis, multilateral trading system and Japan U.S. Relations," in Japan's Post Gulf International Initiatives (Japan: Ministry of Foreign Affairs, August 1991), p.20.

29. FOF August 31, 1990.

30. FOF Nov. 16, 1990.

31. FOF August 24, 1990.

32. Ibid.

33. FOF Nov. 16, 1990; FOF Jan. 19, 1990.

34. FOF Jan. 10, 1991.

35. FOF Dec. 15, 1989.

36. Katzenstein op. cit., pp. 106-107.

37. An article by Israel Prime Minister Yitzhak Rabin published in *Japan Times*, Dec. 13th, 1994.

38. *Japan Times*, Dec. 13. An interview with Amos Ganor, Ambassador of Israel to Japan.

39. *Japan Times*, Dec. 14th, 1994.

40. *Japan Times*, Dec. 13th, 1994.

41. *Japan Times*, Dec. 7th, 1994. An article by Hisane Masaki Japan Times, Dec. 13th, 1994.

42. *Japan Times*, Dec. 14th, 1994.

43. Ibid.

44. *Japan Times*, Dec. 13,1994.

45. Ibid. About Japanese cultural heritage, see Kazuo Ogura, "The role of culture in Japan's Foreign Policy," in *Japan Times*, July 6, 1991, and *Japan's Post Gulf International Initiatives*, pp. 33-36.

46. *Japan Times*, Dec. 15th, 1994.

47. Hisane Masaki, "Japan strives to define its role on world stages," *Japan Times,* Jan. 1st, 1995.

48. Nye, op.cit,. pp. 98-99.

49. Funabashi, op.cit,. p. 28.

50. Katzenstein, op. cit., p. 84; Berger, op. cit., p. 148 ; Funahashi, op. cit., p. 32.

51. Nye, op.cit., pp. 98-99.

52. *Japan Times*, Dec. 21st,1994. ODA totaled ¥109 trillions; there is a trend to lessen it because of Japan tight fiscal conditions.

53. Ako Washio, "Japan dragging its heels on U.N. peacekeeping," *Japan Times*, Jan. 3rd, 1995.

54. Nye, op. cit., p. 112.

55. Ibid.

56. See "Japan should look to its future in Asia," *Japan Times*, Jan. 4th, 1995.

57. Masaki, op. cit.

CHAPTER 13

Trend of Italian Studies in the Arab World

I tried to follow Italian studies in the Arab quarterlies and to explore what their concentration was over twenty-five years. It was a surprise to find very few studies. Among the Arab quarterlies, I found one quarterly that published studies about the Italian affairs in the Arab world, the Egyptian quarterly *Al Siyassa Al Dawliyya* (AA), published in Arabic by the Political and Strategic Studies Center Al Ahram in Cairo, Egypt. The first issue appeared in 1965. It is the most famous periodical in the Middle East according to the level of its writers, who belong to the elites of intellectuals of the Arab world. They are mainly from Cairo University. Over thirty years there were twenty-four studies about Italian issues. The writers concentrated on internal Italian affairs such as elections and political crises. We can follow the studies about Italy as follows. Before 1970 there were no studies about Italy. During the period 1970–1975 five studies appeared and concentrated on Italian affairs. Two studies concentrated on the war between Italy and Ethiopia during the years 1935–1936. One of the studies revealed that Egyptian public opinion was against Italy. The studies concentrated a lot on the relationship between the two churches in Egypt and Ethiopia. Moreover, Egyptians were worried because the Italian forces' occupation may have affected the trbutaries of the Nile River. 90% of the Nile tributaries come from the basin in Ethiopia.

Egyptian Support

The studies revealed that Egypt was ready to fight against the Italians in Ethiopia. Public opinion was against Italian occupation for several reasons—the water and the historical roots of relations between Ethiopia and Islam when the prophet Mohammad sent seventy Moslems to Naghashi, the ruler of Ethiopia, at the dawn of Islam. He welcomed and protected them. The concentration on this subject in the press increased the hatred against Italians. The press itself participated in escalating the hatred against Italy. Publishing certain events was a great factor in increasing the hatred; for example, when an Italian jet fighter fired on the Egyptian hospital in Ethiopia, there were riots in the streets and some Italians in Egypt were exposed to the reaction of the demonstrators. The Egyptian government watched and controlled the activities of the Italian minorities in Egypt.

Something attracted my attention in this study—that the Egyptian citizens whose mothers are from Ethiopia became popular personalities. The people sympathized with them. The second study concentrated on the crisis in the Italian government and on the structure of the government in Italy. The third study concentrated on the presidential elections. The fourth study was about Italian foreign policy in the Middle East. It concentrated on Italian interests in the Arab world, which was taken into consideration by the Italian foreign minister, Amintore Fanfani. In May 1967, when the crisis started, the press published in detail the discussion in Italian government and Parliament about the situation in the Middle East.

Italy and Peace in the Middle East

On July 6, 1967, Italy supported the peace plan suggested by the Latin American States because it connected the withdrawal from the territories occupied by Israel in the 1967 war and the termination of the war in the Middle East. Italy was the sole state in the Mediterranean that supported the USA and sided with it in the UN. The Communist Party criticized the government for not being able to have a clear position. An excuse may be found for Italy's concentrating on a resolution inside the UN because this resolution would assist Italy to keep its interest in the Middle East. Any resolution outside the UN may have caused the Italian interst in the Middle East to be ignored. In short, the Italian position between June 1967 and December 1968 sided with the USA and Israel on both levels—the government and the people.

New Developments

By 1968, three developments took place. First, the four superpowers in the UN started to hold negotiations outside the UN—the thing that Italy wanted to avoid. Second, the Italian companies especially the ENE started to recognize the loss that resulted from the suspension of the Suez Canal. Third, the escalation on the war of attrition between the Arabs and the Israelis.

A new trend in Italian foreign policy appeared. This trend reflected an independent Italian position away from the USA position. On July 9, 1969, for the first time the Italian foreign minister, who belonged to the socialist party and who was noted for sympathizing with Israel, changed his attitude and demanded a balanced situation in the Middle East. The Italian government criticized the four superpowers—the US, UK, France, and USSR—who started to discuss Middle East issues outside the UN. The Italian government suggested forming a committee from the four superpowers and six states-three from the eastern bloc and three from the western bloc. Italy was looking for a role, taking into consideration that she was the most important and the closest to the Arab world of the Mediterranean European states. The Arab capitals received Italian delegations offering suggestions and showing eagerness to reach a settlement reflecting neutrality in the Middle East dispute.

In May 1970, the Italian foreign minister headed a delegation to Egypt. There he assured the Italian interest to have a peaceful and just settlement. A few days later he expressed his worries about the security in the Mediterranean Sea and the threat from the Israeli occupation of the Arab territories. In the first six months of 1971, the deputy of the Italian foreign minister visited Beirut, Damascus, and Baghdad, where he concentrated on the idea that peace in the Middle East is a priority to all the Mediterranean states and not the four superpowers only. The Italian leaders clarified that the Italian role was not the role of mediator, but to help clarify the different points of view of the two sides in the Middle East. The Italian Position changed between June 1967 and the early seventies. The Italian Position in 1967 concentrated on the humanitarian side of the conflict, but in the early seventies several Italian parties started to talk about the refugees' rights.

Suez Canal Opening

The opening of the Suez Canal was a priority for the Italians. Italy felt that the Mediterranean had become a lake like it was in the 19th century, and Italy felt the Americans were not interested in opening the canal. In June 1969, Italian Prime Minister Mariano Roomer sought Turkish Support to open the canal. When the peace initiative of the American Secretary of the State Mr. Rogers appeared in 1970, Italy supported it. In April 1973, the Italian Prime Minister discussed the opening of the Suez Canal with American President Nixon and the Secretary General of the UN. Italy offered economic assistance to the Arab States, especially Egypt. Italy offered Egypt assistance to widen the canal. In short, Italy started to have an independent point of view toward the conflict in the Middle East that diverged from the American point of view. Facing the pressure of the political parties inside Italy to continue in an independent policy from the Americans, Italy mobilized its efforts inside the EEC.

The Trend of Other Studies

The trend of the other studies in the periodical mentioned above concentrated mainly on the internal affairs in Italy as following:

1. Between 1976 and 1979, six studies concentrated on the elections, stability, and internal issues.
2. Between 1981 and 1985, five studies appeared and concentrated on political developments, violence, and the future of Euro communism in Italy.
3. Between 1987 and 1992, two studies concentrated on the Italian elections.
4. Between 1993 and 1999, six studies concentrated on political crises In Italy.

In summary, there were few concentrations on Italian studies in the Arabic periodicals. The studies mentioned above did not reflect the level of relationship between Italy and the Arabs. One of the studies was about the colonial era of Italy, which reflected negative memories in Egypt, not the Arab world, and the rest were about the peace process in the Middle East. Most of the studies concentrated on Italian political affairs like the internal crisis and the elections. The scope of these studies is very limited in the political and academic fields. In quantity, the number is small. The average is a study every thirteen months. Half of the studies were in the seventies. This may reflect the interest in the Italian affairs in that period. Later, the USA's influence after Camp David became greater in Egypt. Egypt's priorities changed.

Notes

1. A. Awdeh, (The Egyptian public opinion and the Ethiopian Italian war) in AA NO. 19 Jan 1970, pp. 40-58.

2. A. Elqarie, (Govt. Crisis in Egypt) in AA NO. 17 July 1970 pp 153-174.

3. N. Ahmad, (Political troubles and elections in Italy.) NO.28 April 1972, pp. 138-148.

4. B. Asfahani, (Italian attitude towards the Middle East) in AA NO. 33 July 1973, pp. 156-163.

5. N. Afandi, (The settlement of Italian political dilemma) in AA NO. 42 Oct 1975, pp. 106-116.

6. N. Afandi (Necessity of changes and the Italian elections) in AA NO. 45 July 1976, pp. 149-154.

7. N. Afandi, (Tempestuous Italy across the Atlantic) in AA NO. 46 Oct 1976, pp. 141-145.

8. H. Saudi, (Italy and political future) in AA NO. 52 April 1978, pp. 160-166.

9. A Mohd, (Italy: two years after elections) in AA NO. 54 Oct 1978, pp. 125-129.

10. T. Macci, (Italy between order and disorder) in AA NO. 56 April 1979, pp. 172-175.

11. M. Anees, (Seminar on Disarmament) in AA NO. 57 July 1979 pp 185-187.

12. N.I. Mahmoud, (Violence and political crisis in Italy) in AA NO 63 Jan 1981, pp. 187-190. There is another study about the development of the terrorism kidnapping by H.A. Bakir inAA No.68 April 1982, pp. 165-169.

13. L.A. Abraham, (Elections and searching for an option) in AA NO. 74 Oct 1983, pp. 177-182.

14. E.A. Othman, (Italy and Euro communism) in AA No. 78 Oct 1984, pp. 180-184.

15. E.A. Othman, (Politcal dilemma in Italy in AA NO. 82 Oct 1985, pp. 203-208.

16. A.Salman, (Italy and elections) in AA NO. 90 Oct 1987, pp. 227-231.

17. A. Shokri, (Italian elections) in AA NO. 169 July 1992, pp. 265-271.

18. N. Afandi, (Italian political crisis! To where) in AA NO. 113 July 1993, pp. 182-193.

19. N. Afandi, (Italy between stability and crisis) in AA NO. 131 April 1998, pp. 280-283.

20. S. Hussein, (Italy and new historical era) in AA NO. 117 July 1994, pp. 235-242.

21. S. Hussein, (The Italian right and the difficult choice) in AA No. 119 Jan 1995, pp. 197 202.

22. S. Hussein, (Italy from reverse to reverse) in AA NO. 125 July 1996, pp.

163-167.

23. R. M. Kamil, (Italy and the new crisis for the leftist Govt) in AA NO. 135 Jan 1999, pp. 238-233.

About the Author

Professor Saad AbuDayeh is a graduate of Penn State University. He started his career as diplomat in the Jordanian Foreign Office, and later joined Jordan University as a Political Science Professor. He was a visiting professor in Nagoya University, Japan, and in the Middle East Centre St. Anthony College Oxford–UK. Author of 50 books and more than 40 papers about Jordanian and Arab issues, he was awarded a Medal of the Independence by King Abdullah II and awarded by the University of Jordan the prize for best researcher.

Mailing address:
P.O. Box, 13655 Amman 11942 Jordan
Email: abudayeh@hotmail.com

Related Titles from Westphalia Press

The Limits of Moderation: Jimmy Carter and the Ironies of American Liberalism

The Limits of Moderation: Jimmy Carter and the Ironies of American Liberalism is not a finished product. And yet, even in this unfinished stage, this book is a close and careful history of a short yet transformative period in American political history, when big changes were afoot.

The Zelensky Method
by Grant Farred

Locating Russian's war within a global context, The Zelensky Method is unsparing in its critique of those nations, who have refused to condemn Russia's invasion and are doing everything they can to prevent economic sanctions from being imposed on the Kremlin.

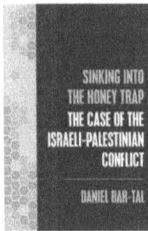

Sinking into the Honey Trap: The Case of the Israeli-Palestinian Conflict
by Daniel Bar-Tal, Barbara Doron, Translator

Sinking into the Honey Trap by Daniel Bar-Tal discusses how politics led Israel to advancing the occupation, and of the deterioration of democracy and morality that accelerates the growth of an authoritarian regime with nationalism and religiosity.

Essay on The Mysteries and the True Object of The Brotherhood of Freemasons
by Jason Williams

The third edition of Essai sur les mystères discusses Freemasonry's role as a society of symbolic philosophers who cultivate their minds, practice virtues, and engage in charity, and underscores the importance of brotherhood, morality, and goodwill.

Bunker Diplomacy: An Arab-American in the U.S. Foreign Service
by Nabeel Khoury

After twenty-five years in the Foreign Service, Dr. Nabeel A. Khoury retired from the U.S. Department of State in 2013 with the rank of Minister Counselor. In his last overseas posting, Khoury served as deputy chief of mission at the U.S. embassy in Yemen (2004-2007).

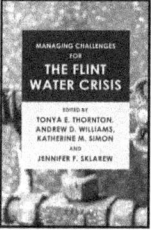

Managing Challenges for the Flint Water Crisis
Edited by Toyna E. Thornton, Andrew D. Williams, Katherine M. Simon, Jennifer F. Sklarew

This edited volume examines several public management and intergovernmental failures, with particular attention on social, political, and financial impacts. Understanding disaster meaning, even causality, is essential to the problem-solving process.

User-Centric Design
by Dr. Diane Stottlemyer

User-centric strategy can improve by using tools to manage performance using specific techniques. User-centric design is based on and centered around the users. They are an essential part of the design process and should have a say in what they want and need from the application based on behavior and performance.

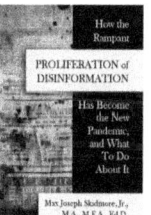

How the Rampant Proliferation of Disinformation Has Become the New Pandemic, and What To Do About It by Max Joseph Skidmore Jr.

This work examines the causes of the overwhelming tidal wave of fake news, misinformation, disinformation, and propaganda, and the increase in information illiteracy and mistrust in higher education and traditional, vetted news outlets that make fact-checking a priority.

Abortion and Informed Common Sense
by Max J. Skidmore

The controversy over a woman's "right to choose," as opposed to the numerous "rights" that abortion opponents decide should be assumed to exist for "unborn children," has always struck me as incomplete. Two missing elements of the argument seems obvious, yet they remain almost completely overlooked.

The Athenian Year Primer: Attic Time-Reckoning and the Julian Calendar
by Christopher Planeaux

The ability to translate ancient Athenian calendar references into precise Julian-Gregorian dates will not only assist Ancient Historians and Classicists to date numerous historical events with much greater accuracy but also aid epigraphists in the restorations of numerous Attic inscriptions.

Siddhartha: Life of the Buddha
by David L. Phillips,
contributions by Venerable Sitagu Sayadaw

Siddhartha: Life of the Buddha is an illustrated story for adults and children about the Buddha's birth, enlightenment and work for social justice. It includes illustrations from Pagan, Burma which are provided by Rev. Sitagu Sayadaw.

Growing Inequality: Bridging Complex Systems, Population Health, and Health Disparities
Editors: George A. Kaplan, Ana V. Diez Roux, Carl P. Simon, and Sandro Galea

Why is America's health is poorer than the health of other wealthy countries and why health inequities persist despite our efforts? In this book, researchers report on groundbreaking insights to simulate how these determinants come together to produce levels of population health and disparities and test new solutions.

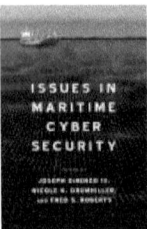

Issues in Maritime Cyber Security
Edited by Dr. Joe DiRenzo III, Dr. Nicole K. Drumhiller, and Dr. Fred S. Roberts

The complexity of making MTS safe from cyber attack is daunting and the need for all stakeholders in both government (at all levels) and private industry to be involved in cyber security is more significant than ever as the use of the MTS continues to grow.

Female Emancipation and Masonic Membership: An Essential Collection
By Guillermo De Los Reyes Heredia

Female Emancipation and Masonic Membership: An Essential Combination is a collection of essays on Freemasonry and gender that promotes a transatlantic discussion of the study of the history of women and Freemasonry and their contribution in different countries.

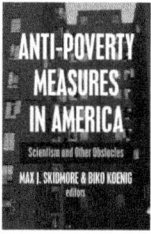

Anti-Poverty Measures in America: Scientism and Other Obstacles
Editors, Max J. Skidmore and Biko Koenig

Anti-Poverty Measures in America brings together a remarkable collection of essays dealing with the inhibiting effects of scientism, an over-dependence on scientific methodology that is prevalent in the social sciences, and other obstacles to anti-poverty legislation.

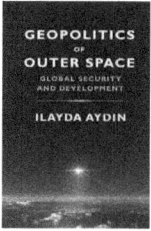

Geopolitics of Outer Space: Global Security and Development
by Ilayda Aydin

A desire for increased security and rapid development is driving nation-states to engage in an intensifying competition for the unique assets of space. This book analyses the Chinese-American space discourse from the lenses of international relations theory, history and political psychology to explore these questions.

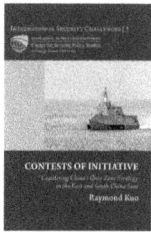

Contests of Initiative: Countering China's Gray Zone Strategy in the East and South China Seas
by Dr. Raymond Kuo

China is engaged in a widespread assertion of sovereignty in the South and East China Seas. It employs a "gray zone" strategy: using coercive but sub-conventional military power to drive off challengers and prevent escalation, while simultaneously seizing territory and asserting maritime control.

Discourse of the Inquisitive
Editors: Jaclyn Maria Fowler and Bjorn Mercer

Good communication skills are necessary for articulating learning, especially in online classrooms. It is often through writing that learners demonstrate their ability to analyze and synthesize the new concepts presented in the classroom.

westphaliapress.org

Policy Studies Organization

The Policy Studies Organization (PSO) is a publisher of academic journals and book series, sponsor of conferences, and producer of programs.

Policy Studies Organization publishes dozens of journals on a range of topics, such as European Policy Analysis, Journal of Elder Studies, Indian Politics & Polity, Journal of Critical Infrastructure Policy, and Popular Culture Review.

Additionally, Policy Studies Organization hosts numerous conferences. These conferences include the Middle East Dialogue, Space Education and Strategic Applications Conference, International Criminology Conference, Dupont Summit on Science, Technology and Environmental Policy, World Conference on Fraternalism, Freemasonry and History, and the Internet Policy & Politics Conference.

For more information on these projects, access videos of past events, and upcoming events, please visit us at:

www.ipsonet.org

Λ